The Grumpy Middle Aged Dad - Adventures In Orlando

MICHAEL HADLEY

Grumpy Middle-Aged Dad – Adventures In Orlando

Copyright © Michael Hadley 2017

From the Author: -

I have tried to recreate events, locales, incidents and conversations from my memories of them. In order to maintain their anonymity in some instances I have changed the names of individuals and places, I may have changed some identifying characteristics and details such as physical properties, occupations and places of residence. Any names or characters, businesses or places, events or incidents, are fictitious. Any resemblance to actual persons, living or dead, or actual events is purely coincidental.

All proceeds from this book were donated to charity. I did not make a single penny from this book – if you have reason to be offended, please don't sue me.

Michael Hadley, The Black Country, 2017

To Catherine, Sam and Lottie.

Thanks for putting up with me, love you all xxx

Reviews for The Grumpy Middle-Aged Dad Blog

Facebook- @grumpymiddleageddadblog

"I'm still crying with laughter from reading the down to earth, side splitting funny blogs. This will brighten anybody's day" – Sara-Jane Tuckwood

"This guy is hilarious I don't just mean funny I mean side splitting nose snotting can't catch breath hilarious. Please read his tell it how it is blog on Florida." – Maria Elam Peppiatt

"Literally been in absolute stiches reading these blogs!! At times in the worst places! Fantastic, cannot wait for the book" – Laura Barham

"Grumpy is hysterical! I absolutely love reading his blogs and thoughts about everything! During his recent visit to Orlando, I would read the blogs and literally laugh out loud! Great blog with an excellent writing style! I hope he keeps it up. Thanks Grumpy for the great entertainment. A USA friend" – Erin Elliot

"Can you hurry up and finish this sodding book as you're getting on my nerves now" – Wifey

"Anyone who has been to Disneyworld in Orlando will relate to this hilarious day by day blog. I couldn't stop reading about his everyday adventures - it is so funny I

even had my husband enthralled, that in itself says it all!"
– Lynda Vernon

"Side splitting blogs!! Loved his quick witted humour and for saying what most of us are feeling" – JoJo Parker

"Grumpy Middle-Aged Dad is laugh out loud, spit your tea out funny. I couldn't wait to read the next instalment of what he and "The Fam" got up to in Orlando. Clever wit and absolutely hilarious" – Amanda Graham

Grumpy Middle-Aged Dad – Adventures in Orlando

Contents

Acknowledgements

Genuine, heartfelt Grumpy thanks go to everyone that commented on the original blogs and encouraged me to keep going, to the many Grumpys and Grumpettes that came forward with help and advice, to all the incredible team at "It's Orlando Time" Facebook group for their help, encouragement and support, Amanda Stedman for the proof reading and managing to overlook my outbursts of Black Countary (ta bab), and to Alison May for the real grown up stuff like learning me how to actually write a book an stuff.

Thanks to all at both The Neuro Foundation and Follow Your Dreams – these people really are superhuman and deserve so much more than they get.

Special mention to Debbie from Guildford, Agnes from Cleethorpes and Babs from Bristol who all think I'm hilarious.

And finally to The Fam, without whom I would have never have sodding gone to Orlando in the first place. I love all three of you more than you could ever know and thanks for not laughing.

The Brainfart

It's a tough life, being a Grumpy Middle-Aged Dad.

I have no idea why, but the onset of Middle Age seems to bring with it a whole host of new ways for the world to wind you up.

Every day presents a new challenge, whether it be unexpected and totally pointless roadworks on your way to work, a particularly thick shop assistant or simply another broken hand dryer, there are a huge amount of adversities to face that would make any normal sane bloke turn quickly in to a ranting looney.

And, trust me on this, it's even tougher when you're a Grumpy Middle-Aged Dad in the Black Country.

There must be something in the water that makes us Black Country folk just that bit more miserable than others. Maybe Black Country water is pumped directly from the myriad of canals (or "cuts" as they're known, as in "cut in to the ground") and over the decades we've all been infected by seeping chemicals from rusty Ford Cortinas, abandoned Tesco shopping trollies and thousands of unwanted Slade LPs.

Or maybe it's just the history of the place that gives us the nod as the grumpiest place in Britain. For you lucky readers that don't know this area, I should point out that the Black Country is a non-defined part of the West Midlands, made up of a collection of towns and villages that were made famous during the industrial revolution for belching out black smoke from factory chimneys and the miners emerging from pits covered head to toe in black soot - hence "The Black Country".

The area is world renowned as the birthplace of heavy industry during the Industrial Revolution – ironworks, foundries, chain makers, coal mining, and in addition all the spin off manufacturing and service industries. Towns in the Black Country such as Dudley, West Bromwich, Tipton, Bilston all had their own identities depending on that areas specific industry and would even have their own dialect. Black Country people are tough and real "salt of the earth" types that revel in hard work and have strong family values.

And love moaning.

There is just something in the Black Country DNA that makes us enjoy a good grumble. Whether it's the price of a sodding pint, the fact there's nothing on the bloody telly, the cost of a God taxi or just the weather, we can find misery in everything and for an outsider it must be really difficult to comprehend.

It's not so much as the glass is half full or half empty, more like "which buggers nicked me glass?".

My personal theory (I have a lot of these) is that it stems from all the years when Black Country folk were packed off to work in the factories and sent down the mines, leaving a decades long legacy of miserable buggers who were raised in desolation and therefore spent most the time griping and moaning about their fate.

But God did bless us with the perfect accent for moaning. If you don't know the Black Country accent, imagine the Brummie accent but even slower, thicker and slightly more retarded. Sort of Jasper Carrot trying to perform live on sleeping tablets.

Even the nicest, heartfelt compliment given in a Black Country accent sounds completely insincere and sarcastic.

Try this in your normal voice:

"Ooh that dress looks lovely on, darling"

Now try like this as Benny from Crossroads mixed with Noddy Holder, speaking whilst having open brain surgery:

"Yow luk reaallay, reaallay, luverlaaaaay in that frock bab, yow reaallly dooo …."

Over the decades, the Black Country suffered tremendously due to the fall in demand for our resources, many recessions and bad or no planning to replace jobs and infrastructure by successive governments. Despite these adversaries, we soldier on and find new ways to make a living and uphold the traditions of hard work and moaning.

The Black Country is where my heart is – it's home to all my family, where I was born and brought up and where I live and work. I wouldn't change it for a thing.

Actually, that's totally not true, I would change it if I could.

If I had a chance, I'd live in Monte Carlo sleeping on a big pot of cash spending my days on a yacht surrounded by beautiful women. Instead, I live near Dudley, I'm skint, the closest thing to a yacht I'll get is a barge on the canal and most women in The Black Country are more manly than men.

In order to get a break from the monotony and daily drudge of everyday life, Black Country folk occasionally set off to other parts of the world on holiday. This gives us the chance to complain about <u>their</u> weather, <u>their</u> food and the price of <u>their</u> funny tasting pint in a different country where they all talk funnier than we do loike.

Some Black Country folk choose to holiday in the UK, and you will often find thousands of them populating the B & B's and caravan parks of the Welsh coast, with Barmouth and Aberdovey as particular favourites. Other Black Country folk have broadened their horizons as the world has become a smaller place and decided to go even further afield, so it's not unusual to see the good old Black Country flag being waved from exotic places like the top of Sydney Harbour Bridge or in front of The Petronas Towers.

And then some Black Country folk think they still need a passport to get into Poundland, so personally I think they should just be locked indoors.

Our Fam has no particular favourite holiday destination, and tend to try new things. I've learnt that so long as there's stuff to do, nice food to eat and the kids are happy, it doesn't really matter.

At this point, please let me introduce you to The Fam who go on to play a starring role in this book and without whom I would have had naff all to moan about.

The Fam is made up of three component parts – Wifey, Teenage Son and Teenage Daughter

Me and Wifey have been together for….. erm,…. ages. About 20 something years? I lose count. Anyway, we met when we were both slim, fresh faced and enthusiastic about life and once we eventually decided we were on to a good thing (and just before she realised that I was punching *way* above my weight) decided to tough it out together and buy a house in the Black Country.

Teenage son came along after 6 blissfully carefree years, closely followed by Teenage Daughter just 20 months after (there was a happy two-week window between Wifey being post-natally depressed with Son and pre-natally depressed with Daughter. Bullseye! Top shootin' by Grumpy if I do say so meself)

We both work, me as a Grumpy Managing Director of a car parts company in Dudley and Wifey as a fully-fledged Podiatrist, and as I write this fabulous book, both teenage kids are at a college somewhere, studying something. By the time this is published, they will both have finished college and be off doing a job somewhere and good luck to them with that.

We are no different to any other Fam and probably have the same worries and concerns as most Fams – work, college, money, cars, parents….. you name it, the kind of stuff you go through dear reader is no different to ours and every other warm, brightly lit household up and down the country.

As for me, I am Grumpy almost all of the time, and especially Grumpy when I get home from work having had to spend my entire day slogging my guts out in a tough industry with moaning customers, unreliable suppliers and a cretinous Black Country workforce. However, the Grumpiness tends to subside around 6 o clock, when tea is consumed, feet put up and a very large gin and tonic sits seductively next to a Kinder Bueno and the remote control.

As the gin anaesthetises my senses just enough to absorb Wifey's Alan Titchmarsh programmes, I find myself the happiest I've been all day, with the woes and worries of my job fading into memory just long enough for me to forget I've got to go back there again tomorrow.

It was during one of these happy-cum-dopey moments surrounded by The Fam in late 2016 that I had a Brainfart.

A Brainfart is a sudden, temporary mental lapse or failure to reason correctly, sometimes leading to a snap decision by a person who under normal circumstances would stop and carefully consider what the fuck he or she was doing.

Small examples of a Brainfart would be things like putting the cups in the fridge rather than the cupboard…… putting moisturiser in your hair and hair gel on your face…… walking out to your car and realising you don't have the keys. Or a car.

I've done all of the above.

However, as you get older and supposedly wiser, Brainfarts tend to rise from small, inconsequential acts of thoughtlessness to life changing acts of complete cockwomblery.

The Brainfart that I'm leading up to involves the booking of the Fam's trip to see Mr Disney again. We had already agreed that we wouldn't go back to see him after the last trip in 2013, as we couldn't possibly top the experience we'd had. Well, that's what I'd convinced them all to think after I realised that it was going to take two years to pay off my credit card bill.

But it was a cold mid-October day, 6 o clock and already dark outside and we were all a bit fed up. I was already halfway down a big glass of Bombay Sapphire when Mr Disney broadcast one of his heart tugging adverts – you know the one where he shows you magical images of happy kids, smiling handsome dads and fit soccer mums, all enjoying themselves in the sunshine surrounded by a giggling Mickey and Donald.

In these adverts, Mr Disney also does something *really* clever by hooking you in to a cunning financial scheme he's got going on. Mr Disney has this Dining Plan whereby if you pay him early enough the year before your holiday, he gives you a load of free food on some bewildering credits based system (much, much more of that later) and your holiday includes entrance to all of Mr Disney's Psychedelic Parks.

My telly didn't show the *real-life* Mr Disney advert - the advert that shows hot, bad tempered kids having a tantrum, sweaty bedraggled mums arguing with pissed off skint dads about the Dining Plan, all being cajoled into having a picture taken with grown men dressed as animals.

Perhaps if Mr Disney had shown THAT advert, I wouldn't have done what I did……..

PPPFffffFFFFFFFFaaaAAARRRTTT………. Pfft….

The Brainfart was over in a matter of mind boggling moments. All I can remember is that one minute I'm sitting in my armchair, swigging gin, eating chocolate and calling Alan Titchmarsh a prick and the next my naughty credit card had spunked £5 grand on two weeks at Mr Disney's Beach Club Resort and another £2 grand on 4 seats on a British Airways flight to Miami and back.

"How did that happen?", I asked myself.

"That, my chubby friend, was a Brainfart. And a stonking good one…." the voice inside my head answered.

"Ya prick" he added (I think I'd had too much gin)

Anyway, The Fam were happy and for a brief moment there was a feeling of genuine love and elation in the Grumpy household that was only cut short when Teenagers started rowing again and Alan Titchmarsh turned up on my telly, this time reading the news (I Think. If not I'd definitely had too much gin)

Sobering up over the next 24 hours, I realised that this wasn't just a £7 grand holiday – I'd only really paid to get there and back and for four of us to sleep in a room. On the horizon ahead there lay many more great and expensive adventures like shopping malls, posh meals out and cabarets. And there was likely to be a "break" from spending time with Mr Disney by popping over to see his nemesis and long-lost cousin, Mr Universal, and any other number of Orlando tourist traps involving roller coasters and alligators.

All these worries were laying heavy on my pocket, so I resigned myself to cutting back on the gin and Chinese take-aways, cancelling Netflix, all the Porn channels and Sky Sports and vowing to save as much cash as possible before the day came next year when I had to go to The Money Shop and change my hard-earned wages for Disney Dollars. And / Or sell Wifey's designer handbags and put Teenage Kids on E-Bay.

The next nine months' wait dragged on and on and on, punctuated by seemingly countless elections, hundreds of TV appearances by Nigel Farage and Wolverhampton Wanderers having 4 managers. We had Halloween (Pointless!) Bonfire Night (Noisy!) and Christmas (Total Grumpfest, worthy of a book all by itself!).

One of the elections bought my old mate Donald Trumpet on to the world stage as America's 45th President and Leader of the Free World, an historical moment that my Grumpy old brain still can't fathom and has turbo charged my Grumpiness to a whole new transatlantic level. What a world we were living in!

And don't start me on Brexit…… FFS…..

Anyway, soon the time had arrived when dusty suitcases were hoisted down from the loft and the last ten years' worth of summer holiday clothes were unpacked and laid out on the bed. Then followed the annual tradition of looking longingly at summer holiday clothes that once adorned a slimmer version of myself – designer polos, tight shirts, short shorts – a whole wardrobe of clothes that at some point in time both fitted and suited the skinny version of me that did once exist.

These precious garments, some still with labels on, were held aloft like Excalibur as I dreamed of days gone by where I didn't look like a human blob. The annual tradition continued with several failed attempts at shoehorning my blubbery body into various shirts, skinny shorts and tight t-shirts in the vain attempt that somehow I could reverse belly gravity by standing up straight.

After eventually accepting the inevitable, losing my temper and shouting into the mirror through chubby tears "it's your own fault ya fat bastard. Stop eating!", I picked up all the popped buttons and returned summer holiday clothes to their rightful place back up the loft (Well, I'm not going to throw them away am I? They'll fit next year when I've lost some weight….)

Brainfart forgotten, the countdown was into single days……

The pre-holiday diet abandoned as it was too late to make any difference.

The trip to The Money Shop complete at an appalling exchange rate.

Increased security measures were in place to deter nasty burglars.

Neighbours, family were informed of our absence.

Suitcases were rammed shut with stuff we wouldn't need.

Dog packed off to the neighbour with enough food to feed a small dog-petting zoo.

Wifey hoovered the house one last time as the rest of us sat in the loaded-up car.

The time had come (albeit 30 minutes after the agreed, designated time I told Wifey we needed to leave)

We were off!

The Flight

Before I can start to enjoy my time in Orlando, however, I need to get there. And that means going on a plane.

I don't like planes.

No, actually that's not true – I like planes but only when they are looking shiny, silent and broody whilst sitting on the tarmac. And I suppose when they're in the air doing their flighty thing they're also cool........so long as I'm not in it.

It just doesn't make sense to me that this great big heavy thing can get in the air. Hundreds of people, tons of luggage, litre upon litre of cheap duty free... the weight of the trolley dollys' make up alone is enough to tether a big hot air balloon. Yet it still gets up, up and away into the sky (almost) every time and providing the engine doesn't suck up a nearby unsuspecting goose, you can be anywhere in the world within a few bumpy hours.

I've learnt to address and confront my fear of flying by using my own, self-taught coping mechanism, which is essentially half a bottle of vodka and tranquilisers.

Now I'm not advocating the use of drugs or alcohol, I'm really not. But you see the problem is I'm a complete and utter scaredy cat when it comes to flying and depending on where I am or where I'm going I sometimes need a little soothener to take the edge of proceedings.

I also have a load of pre-flight superstitions that I have to follow before I can convince myself that the next time my family will see my chubby body won't be through dental records. I have to be at the airport at least three hours before a flight. I must buy at least one thing from duty free. I must poo and wee twice before I leave. And I have to be pissed.

But most importantly, I have to make sure I have my goodbye text ready to send to Wifey (I also have this in paper form in my top pocket, but I'm assuming I will be burnt to a crisp so best to be safe). So, if an important piece of the plane goes whizzing past the window and we begin to nosedive into planet Earth, I can quickly turn off airplane mode and send this:

Wifey

If I die in a plane crash, this is the last thing I want you to remember....

I love you.

With all of my heart and soul. And with every fibre of my being.

You are my morning sunshine, my daily drive and my last thought before I sleep.

You have brought me life's riches and happiness beyond my imagination and I am truly humbled that you have chosen me to share your existence here on earth.

Without you, my life would be unfulfilled and incomplete....

I love you. In this life and the next.

If they find my body, donate all of my organs.

Except the penis. Which you can choose to keep, or donate it to the Natural History Museum

Love you, Michael

I'm not entirely sure what started my fear of flying but I'm pretty sure the root of the problem was on a flight back from my first trip to Disney in Orlando with my mum, dad and sister when I was about 11 and looked dead cute (I really was cute. I mean like uber cute)

This was in the reckless 1970's when you could still smoke on a plane, which seems like the dark ages now.

It turns out that my dear old dad had a real fear of flying so as soon as the No Smoking light went off and the drop down film screen was set up, he shot straight down the back of the plane with his flares swishing from side to side to spark up Benson and Hedges fags and drink rough scotch....which is pretty much where he stayed for the rest of the flight. There was one particular moment that's been etched on to my brain and is almost certainly the single reason for my own fears now.

My mum had tried and failed to persuade him to get back

to his seat as he was having waaay too much fun with the stewardesses, so she played the kiddy card and sent me and my equally cute little sister down to the back of the plane to use our puppy dog eyed, blonde haired routine to pull him by his heart strings back to his little family.

It didn't work.

As we were coming in to land, I distinctly remember seeing my beloved dad through the haze of 40 B & H, being prised away from the emergency exit by two trolley dolleys. A gibbering, Bells filled wreck, he was hanging on to that big emergency handle for grim life and only staggered back to his seat when a big male steward turned up with a cosh (as I said, this was the reckless 1970's)

And that's the image of flying now imprinted on to my brain. My Dad. My hero. Everything I wanted to be when I grew up. Frightened as a little boy, trapped on a plane totally and utter helpless. It's stuck with me forever.

So fast forward to the here and now and I'm my Dad, with my own little crew to parent and guide through the joys of spending hours trapped in a metal smarties tube, being unceremoniously bumped up and down by Captain Poshtwat and inhaling everyone else's farts.

So to ease me through this, I now rely on a heady cocktail of vodka and prescription tranquilisers to get me through even the shortest of flights. It does turn me into the most ridiculously happy person you have ever met, in stark contrast to the usual grumpy bugger reserved for the rest of my sane and sober life. Believe me, when I'm not higher than a giraffe's nuts I really am a miserable sod. I can be irritated at the slightest thing, annoyed by almost everyone I meet and quickly exasperated by the sheer stupidity of...... aaarghhh.....stuff. I'm mildly annoyed even writing this.

Imagine the contrast when I've taken a mild tranquiliser chased down by a few vodka apple juices – it truly is a sight to behold and as equally impressive as the transformation from Lou Ferringo to the Hulk. Or, more apt in my physical case, like when Mr Benn used to quickly change costume. I stagger on to any plane as happy as a little king, rosy cheeked and with my head bobbing about like a loose shirt button.

Unlike in my real life, I'm chatty, outgoing, **very** interesting and develop a level of intellect that only really unearths itself once I'm truly smacked off my tits. I seem to know an **awful** lot of stuff on a myriad of subjects and be **really** well connected to celebrities when I'm in this state.

I suspect I'm a joy to be with.

The Fam have cottoned on to this phenomenon and quite like the fact that Grumpy lapses into a softer, more pliable version of himself near the expensive stuff in duty free. Clever buggers, these lot. Any trip to the airport is an opportunity for them to buy the latest designer gear or get that expensive bottle of perfume by Katy Perry. Every family flight always results in Drunken Grumpy wafting £20 notes around in duty free like some excitable businessman in a strip club, sending them off to buy "warreva ya want me babby, cos ah luv ya….. hic"

Anyway, back to the here and now and we've made it through check-in, security and the usual palava of airport people moving and ready to set off on another once in a lifetime holiday. The flight and the rest of the journey was fairly mundane to be honest so I'm not going to bore you with any of that and skip straight to the good stuff…… Orlando!

Ready kids? Let's go……

Housekeeping and Grumpy's Glossary

Woah, there.... Just hang on a darn moment.

I reckon I'll have to point out a few basic things before you carry on and get to the good, juicy stuff.

(This part of the book is the equivalent of the pre-flight safety check – ultimately necessary and very much there for your own good. Trust me, if you don't read the following nuggets of information, many of the hilarious jokes are going to be lost on you and you will have wasted your money, and I'd feel terrible about that. But it would be your own fault and you would only have yourself to blame).

Sit up straight and pay attention.

Doors to manual and cross check.

Grumpy Middle-Aged Dad– Adventures in Orlando was written as a ***blog*** (diary for the older readers) whilst on holiday in sunny Florida, unravelling over 18 fun packed days during the summer of 2017. The motivation for the blogs came from a Facebook page called "It's Orlando Time", a virtual meeting place and forum for visitors to Orlando to share ideas, ask questions, get travel tips and generally swap holiday stories.

And blog.

I've never blogged. During my working day in the Black Country, I've never really felt the urge to be honest. Why should I tell everyone what I'm doing, what I've just eaten or that we just found a dead rat in the canteen? The thought of sitting down and consciously banging on about yourself to a total stranger who may not be slightly interested in what you're saying is a bit lost on me.

Hang on………..

** Ahem **

As you were.

To me, a blog was a self-indulgent way to offload your thoughts and opinions on to an audience who generally don't give a shit. And to be honest, I think that's probably about right for 99% of blogs where substance is seemingly secondary to volume of words, and where the subject matter is only of interest to a very small minority of people and the advertisers who pay the blogger to push their products.

By the way, I hear that Hoar Cross Hall Spa in Staffordshire (just off the A38) is a lovely place to spend a weekend. Especially if you were driven there in a brand new Range Rover Evoque Td4 4WD with the full leather upgrade from Lancaster Range Rover in Wolverhampton. #justsaying

This wasn't exactly the case on "It's Orlando Time" as most readers were absolutely **_fascinated_** that little Teagan had an ice cream today, Gary and Wendy from Halifax bought matching t-shirts and The Burrell family had hilarious trouble getting the petrol cap off their Chevy Thunderbutt. How we all laughed….

Oh, and we were all totally enraptured with the tales of Mr and Mrs McVities' (Gluten Free) Blog where they detailed (and I do mean detailed) all the food they couldn't eat at Disney, which is pretty much all of it.

Of course, I'm being harsh. "It's Orlando Time" is a fabulous resource and over the years it has done amazing things for the members and charities. Every single blog was interesting in its own unique way as it was completely personal. No matter the subject, each blog was written with joy and love in the heart of the writer and even an old cynical bastard like me can see them for what they are – a real life documentary of cherished moments in a wonderfully happy place.

It's just that some were a bit.....boring. No disrespect meant to all my fellow bloggers, but c'mon..... I don't need 2,000 words for someone just to tell me you visited a funfair and ate a tasty doughnut (which is 9 words, by the way). And some were sickly sweet, to the point where I found myself shouting at my own phone... I'll leave that there for a moment.

After a few days in the Orlando heat and finding loads to moan about, I decided it was time for an alternative view to the sugary diet being fed to me from everyone else's accounts, so I decided to do my own thing.

Being from The Black Country, I can't do sickly sweet so mine were more of a "sideways" look at all things Disney / Orlando and pretty quickly my daily blogs seemed to strike a chord with quite a few people who hitherto had probably just sat and grumbled in a grumpy silence.

It was almost as if the readers had been liberated, and all the grumpiness simmering below the surface was given freedom to spew out. Strangers were coming forward with comments about their own previously bottled up thoughts, feelings and pet hates about holidaying in the "Most Magical Place On Earth", according to Mr Disney.

What follows is a day by day account of our holiday, seen through the eyes of a Grumpy Middle-Aged Dad with far too much time and alcohol on his hands.

Enjoy.

Oh, I nearly forgot. You also need to read the Glossary below or most of the book will go over your head (again, it would be your own fault):

Grumpy's Glossary

It's Orlando Time – A fabulous Facebook group which brings Orlando fanatics together into one big happy virtual family. The group is a fantastic resource for all things Orlando, from hotel recommendations, restaurants, advice about attractions and travel tips. I can honestly say The Fam found it mahoosively beneficial while we there, not just financially but also in time saved and corners cut. If you are going to Orlando, take my advice and join the Group. It's fab.

Tat – Short name for all theme park merchandise. All of it is tat. And expensive tat at that.

Steps – As in walking. For some bizarre reason there was an obsession with counting the number of steps taken through the day. I'm told that people were using FitBits and phone apps to measure their paces. I'm sure I heard someone say that they had a Paedometer but not sure why / what they would be measuring in Disney.

Disney App – Ahead of our trip on to Mr Disney's land, we were encouraged to download the Disney App so we can see how long it will take us to queue for each ride. The app allows you to book restaurants, check opening times and bag those all-important Fast Passes (see below). Worryingly, Mr Disney's app only works if you allow him permission to see your location, so effectively he knows where you are, what you're doing and how many dollars you're spending..... Mr Disney is Big Brother.

Magic Bands – When staying on one of Mr Disney's hotels, you are given a widgety, magical wrist band that can open your hotel door, gain access to the parks, buy food at restaurants and purchase tat in shops. It runs up a comprehensive list of all of your actions during your time in Disney, so you can be diametrically profiled. Combined with the Disney App (see above) it also records exactly where you are at any moment on Mr Disney's land. Is it me or should we all be very worried about this.....?

Fast Pass – A cheeky way to beat the queues at Mr Disney's Psychedelic Wonderlands. Simply download the Disney App and you can pre-book your place on one of hundreds of rides, performances and roller coasters. This could cut down a 3 hour wait to all of ten minutes AND you get to look dead smug when you walk past everybody else standing in line.

Fart Bus – Mr Disney has his own Magical fleet of buses that transport resort guests from hotel to Psycho Park. All of these buses have been converted to some form of bio fuel, and I'm sure I read somewhere that some of them work off methane (?). I could be wrong, but I love the thought that the buses could actually be powered by Mr Disney's guests' farts. In Grumpy's brain, I can imagine long vacuum cleaner type pipes connecting all of the loos in the Magic Kingdom directly in to the transport yard of the bus depot, ready to syphon all the precious gases from the waste material. Worst job in the world? The poor Disney guy who has to fish the lumps out.

Disney Dining Plan – I'll try to get this right…. Part of Mr Disney's cunning plan to get you completely hooked is to feed you as much food as possible while you're on his land so you waddle around in some carb-fuelled hallucinogenic state and spend more money on tat. The "Disney Dining Plan" is a point based system where MASSIVE meals are rated as "credits" as follows:

- *Snack* - ice cream, pack of crisps, chocolate, soft drink etc. purchased on the go from many outlets across the resorts and parks

- *Quick Service Meal* – essentially "fast food" stuff, eaten with your own hands, off plastic trays on overcrowded benches surrounded by other people and wasps.

- *Table Service Meal* – A proper sit down, menu type meal where a smiley waitress with far too much happiness in her life comes and takes your order, serves your food, calls you all "guys" and expects a 20% tip for doing her job. These are proper restaurants and usually follow a theme depending on where you are on Mr Disney's land, such as "Yak n Yeti's" (Himalayas = Asian food), "Nine Dragons" (Beijing – Chinese Food) or "The Rose and Crown" (British = Crap Food).

- **_Gourmet Meal_** – Mr Disney also has a few super-duper restaurants that are sooo good you have to use TWO credits per person and the smiley waitresses are extra happy because they get a lot more tips.

Each member of your party gets three credits per day – but you don't have to use them every day and you can save them all for other days. You can also swap some credits for other things. And the credits can be used as a family.

Oh, and it doesn't include booze of any kind, and it doesn't include the 20% tip.

Got it?

Nope, nor me (by the time I understood, it was time to go home)

Free Refills – Another fab scam from Mr Disney. At the start of your holiday, for only $15.00 each you can buy a plastic, refillable cup that you can use to constantly top yourself up with sugary drinks. Each cup comes with a lid and a secret embedded chip which records your sugar intake every time you fill it up. "Free Refill" stations, filled with root beer, coke, lemonade et al, are placed all around Mr Disney's hotels BUT, and here's the clever bit, you can't use them in his Psychedelic Parks where all drinks are about $5 each! Genius!

On each refill station, there's a digital display that shows you how many days' worth of free drinks you have left – I'm sure that Mr Disney starts to add LSD to your drinks as your days run down, just in time for you to spending whatever is left of your holiday cash on tat.

Magic Hours – Mr Disney cranks up his Psychedelic Parks a few hours early on selected days, purely for the benefit of On-site Disney guests. This is very nice of him and allows us all that little bit of extra time to deposit more money in to his bank account.

Pandora – Mr Disney has built an entirely new world in one of his Psychedelic Parks. This one is called "Pandora" – it's inside Animal Kingdom and pays homage to the Oscar winning film, "Avatar". The whole land is <u>full</u> of colour and at night is brightly lit up in neon. There are floating islands, colourful plastic animals, and the most amazing, exotic flowers, with street entertainment supplied by a selection of hippy bands with tom tom drums. Mr Disney must have been totally smacked off his tits when he thought this one up.

Mickey Waffles – Probably the most famous item on any menu in all of Mr Disney's hotels. Mickey Waffles are about 2 inches thick, tough as chamois leather and only really taste like proper food when plastered in Mr Disney's Supercalorificextrasweetyaddedsucrose Maple Syrup. They are usually served as breakfast, accompanied with bacon, sausage and a scone (pronounced "sconN" in this book, none of your posh "scowenN" nonsense here thank you very much). All leftover Mickey Waffles are recycled as footings for future Disney buildings.

Captain Eo – A 3D film / experience featuring Michael Jackson. If you don't know it, it would be difficult to really explain this one as no words of mine could possibly do justice just to how strange this "experience" is, especially in light of the weird stuff surrounding MJ's life. Best go off and Google it whilst sitting down.

Freaky Weather: An Eclipse and an impending Hurricane – Early on in our stay in Orlando, we experienced a pretty spectacular eclipse. You may recall it was the one where Donald Trumpet decided to look directly into the sun…. cock. And right at the end of the holiday, we luckily managed to escape the States before Hurricane Irma made land (no jokes here, it must have been awful)

"Mickey's Not So Scary Halloween Night" or **MNSSHN** – A weekly event, held at The Magic Kingdom which heralds the start of Halloween celebrations. In August. Talk about wringing it out….. (see more on Day 13)

Day 1 – Hollywood Studios

> ➢ Cash spent (including air fare, car hire, hotels) - greater than the national debt of Moldova
> ➢ Calories consumed - 2000 (× 1 Mickey Waffle for breakfast) 3780 (lunch) 4675 (tea)
> ➢ Steps taken - happy × 10, grumpy x 15533

So here we bloody go again.... yet another once in a lifetime holiday (this is the third one in five years). We arrived by hired motor vehicle from Miami late yesterday afternoon. It was too late, and we were too knackered, to visit any of Mr Disney's parks so we made do by slumming around in the hotel.

Our choice of Mr Disney's wide range of fine hotels this time is "The Disney Beach Club Resort" which is part of a collection of hotels all built around a man-made lake (full of alligators) encircled by a pretty wooden boardwalk. There's around 5 hotels around the lake in all, varying from dead posh (The Disney Yacht Club) to a bit shit (Dolphin or Swan Hotels – which are not ACTUAL Mr Disney hotels…. Scandalous bit of Disney trickery going on there)

We're staying at The Beach Club as we couldn't afford the much posher Yacht Club this time around, and the only way we could have enough money to stay at the Ultra Posh Grand Floridian is if I sold my one remaining kidney (I sold the other to pay for our stay at The Yacht Club in 2013)

Mr Disney's Beach Club hotel is ok if you get your kicks in retirement homes. It's got a sort of "Granny Chic" feel about it, without the smell of cabbage and wee. I can see what Mr Disney's trying to do here - each of his hotels has a theme like Pop Century (pop music), Animal Kingdom Lodge (animals, obvs) or The Polynesian (dunno). Our theme is "Wealthy American Codger".

But it shares the same pool and restaurants as the posh Yacht Club, where the staff dress as sailors and you're greeted each day by an Admiral who looks like grandad off Only Fools and Horses, and it's about a grand cheaper so it saved Grumpy having to sell Wifey's jewellery.

Anyhoo, we were kitted out with our Magic Bands after breakfast and soon we were outward bound to spend our first full Magical Day on Mr Disney's vast expanse of Orlando real estate at Hollywood Studios – the park where all the magic of Disney films past and present is captured and rolled in to a mix of rides and roller coasters, parades, shops and restaurants. One minute you could be standing next to a Storm Trooper, then the next being serenaded by a street entertainer from a Vaudeville theatre troupe.

It's a great mixture and always entertaining. It's probably The Fam's favourite park – it's not as big (yet) as the other of Mr Disney's Psychedelic Wonderlands so it's easy to get around, isn't so crowded AND it's the home of Toy Story and the other Pixar stuff.

Wifey loves Pixar.

We have to come to this park first so Wifey can have the compulsory "blart at anything Pixar related" emotional meltdown early on in the holiday. To be honest, we both love the Pixar films - Wifey because it reminds her of the time when the kids were little and snuggly and me because they didn't use to cost me a lot and never answered me back. Aaah, those were the days...

Pretty early on in the day, we are both to be found bawling our eyes out in "Pixar The Musical" a musical presentation played out by an orchestra to a backdrop of Pixar's best moments. Wifey is crying because she's just heard the opening to Randy Newman's wonderful "You've Got A Friend In Me...." and I'm crying because just as the show started I'd checked how much money had gone so far on the Grumpy Dad Spentometer App

As I wailed "No... no more..... I can't take it", Wifey looked over at me through blurred tears with a brief look of empathy. She was crying at the passing of time and the inevitable rites of passage for teenage kids, while I was trying to work out how many toddlers I'd have to knock over if I made a dash for the exit.

In the end I decided to stay put as I didn't fancy becoming the first Grumpy Middle-Aged Dad to be evicted from the park for trampling kids, and also because it would have been a waste of a Fast Pass.

We went on to do the Star Tours ride, Muppets in 3D, which is a proper old skool favourite of mine (the kids hate it, which is a bonus) and finally the Aerosmith Roller Coaster. Now here's one of the wonders of Disney - these guys are on a looped video at the start of the ride, so never seem to age. But in real life, Steven Tyler must be knocking on 70 by now and has skin like an old man's ball bag.

We left the park and I was only *mildly* Grumpy, albeit with chaffing to my inner thighs, sore cankles and about $1 million worse off.

On the way back to The Beach Club, aka "Mr Disney's Rest Home for The Financially Retarded", I realised I'd spent so much money already, I'd now need to work until I'm 70.... hmmmph

Grumpy Middle Aged Dad signing off

■■■

Day 2 – Animal Kingdom

➢ Disney Dining Plan credits used - 6 (I think) and still don't get it.
➢ Calories consumed - 6500 (trying to keep it down so only ate once)
➢ Steps taken - happy x nil, mildly annoyed x 5590, grumpy x mostly
➢ Mosquito bites - me x lots, rest of fam x nil

We were all up early today, which is a minor miracle when you have two teenagers, and after a quick check to make sure Donald Trumpet hadn't burnt the world down overnight, we headed off to Animal Kingdom. Today was a super special day for Disney hotel residents as Mr Disney opens the shutters early for 2 extra "Magic Hours" This certainly is Magic for Mr Disney as it's an extra 120 minutes that he has you in his financial grasp.

It seemed that the entire hotel population had the same idea as us, so when we arrived there was already a huge queue to get through the barriers, a bit like the scenes on Boxing day when they let all those Chinese shoppers through the doors on Oxford Street and they end up scrapping on the floor over a George Foreman grill that's been reduced to a fiver.

The Fam were really hoping to get on the brand new Pandora ride in Avatar Land, but as we got approached there was a kid holding a sign at the back of a massive line of people saying "Queue 3 hours from here". It was only 08.15! The park had only been open 15 minutes!

And all for a ride about bracelets? Am I missing something......?

Anyway, we had a quick poke around Avatar Land and vowed to come back when it wasn't so busy, or if we managed to bag an elusive Fast Pass for the Pandora ride.

I really fancied the idea of seeing some wild animals in their natural habitat, or failing that, looking at some bored gorillas behind glass, so we set off to Pretend Africa. In the rush on the way in, I had forgotten to pick up a park map, so we just followed the heady whiff of African animal poo. If you like scruffy animals and the smell of dung, you will not be disappointed in Pretend Africa. Over the next few hours, we saw an amazing amount of poo from exotic animals from all four corners of Africa. To get the real nostril filling effect, I highly recommend Harambe's Poo Watch, Nafiki's Turd Safari and Mbale's World of Dung Conservation.

I'd give Ngolo Kantes Poowatch a miss though.... or at least 5 minutes.

There followed a whistle stop tour of Pretend Asia, including a humungous meal at an Asian fusion restaurant called Yak 'n' Yeti's, which funnily enough was the noise my belly was making going down the Himalayan Yeti roller coaster 10 minutes later.

We then headed over to Dinoland, a pseudo tropical world filled with tatty looking plastic dinosaurs. I'm fairly certain that some poor Disney executive got fired for not getting the exclusive rights to Jurassic Park.

There was one thing I was particularly looking forward to here in Dinoland. But I was to be disappointed....

Last time we were here, I had an enormous, gigantic BBQ ostrich leg, but they don't seem to sell them anymore. I reckon animal rights must have complained about all the one-legged ostriches left in the wild, so Mr Disney was forced to stop selling them. Or maybe some yowoooge yank choked on a bone. Anyway, I couldn't get my chubby hands on one, hence denying me my Yabbadabbadoo Fred Flintstone impression (wrong park anyway)

We also managed to miss the "Finding Nemo" stage show musical spectacular, so there was no bubble snot sobbing to be had for Wifey today, meaning extra snot for tomorrow.

Instead, I did it for her on Mr Disney's eco- friendly fart fuelled bus back to the hotel, when I realised I'd blown all of my spending money for an entire week in just the first two days.

We capped off a hot and sweaty day with a $10 beer and a $15 monster burger at the ESPN Sports Bar. American sports bars are a real experience and could, on entry, be easily confused for the back section of Currys where they sell all the big telly's. I don't think I've ever seen so many different sports all being played simultaneously, all being played somewhere live at all times of the day. True to form, the food portions are massive, with a burger so big it's held together with a splint through the middle and you would need to open your gob like a pedal bin to take a bite.

Went to bed full, Grumpy and farty. Perfect day....

Grumpy Middle Aged Dad signing off.

Nanu nanu

■■■■■■■■■■■■■■■■■■■■■■■■■■■■■■■■■■■■■■ ■■■

Day 3 – The Water Park

> Calories consumed = several times in excess of calories burnt (although I did have a $10 beer with an orange in it (WTF!) so I'm counting that as a treat AND 1 of me 5 a day)
> Arguments with Wifey - nil
> Arguments with teenage kids - 2 (1 won, 1 lost on Wifey made up rules)
> Grains of Disney sand stuck up me arse - 5 gazillion and still counting.

The day I've been dreading..... The Water Park Day ("Dun Dunn Duuuunnuh....")

Now I used to look more than OK in Speedos and back in my day I'd be cool in giving any of these young 'uns a run for their money in the 6 pack stakes. But having spent more than 30 years hunched over a computer, combined with a diet of mostly fast food and booze has rendered my otherwise flat midriff into what is commonly described as a spare tyre.

To be truthful, mine's more of a tractor tyre than a spacesaver.

When I take my top off, it looks like a cheap German supermarket special offer advert on wholesale lumps of Spam.

With this in mind, I'm not really looking forward to the day at Blizzard Lagoon / Wedgey Falls / Pants Wringing Beach or wherever the fuck I'm being dragged to.

But!

When we arrived, just one sight of the American Middle-Aged Dad with his moobs out left me feeling much better about myself, so the top was whipped off (well, wriggled off in painful squeezes of belly fat) and I strutted around like the only cock in the hen house.

I was feeling ok up to the point where a gaggle of athletic kids ran past, all muscled up with sun tan oil highlighting their amazing tattoos. That's when I realised that:

a) I don't have anywhere near enough tattoos and
b) didn't spend enough (or any) time in the gym.

As I strutted slowly past a couple of tasty looking American Soccer mums, I overheard one of them say "jeez Loretta, I thought the eclipse was Monday"

The top was back on in a flash and wobbles of belly blubber.

Why do middle aged people go to these places?

We don't belong here!!!

We don't look good compared to these kids, sand gets all over your face, in your ears, up your bumhole..... there's nowhere to get comfy, the children's screams go right through your brain and the floors either so hot it would melt your corns or so slippery you fall arse over tit and end up sliding along the man-made shoreline like Shamu beaching for a kipper (Or maybe not - he's dead, isn't he? I heard the Seaworld Whale Burgers were good for months after).

The Fam eventually settled down on a hot dusty spot near the bogs -Teenage Son and Daughter went off to ride the waves after the Tarzan call and slip down as many slides as possible and Wifey slapped on the suntan oil and started to soak up the rays.

Wifey doesn't like to get wet. Or rather she doesn't like to get her hair wet, a phenomenon that I believe is shared by many women the world over in swimming pools and water parks. "Don't get me hair wet!" or "Don't you dare splash me" are the usual cries as soon as we enter the water together.

So, I leave Wifey to her sunshine and did my best Lord Lucan act by magically disappearing to find a quiet corner, from where I could sup expensive but cold beer and sulk for 2 hours. (Grumpy's Top Tip – in places like these, always look for the secret smoking corner. Aaaah, you never get judged in a smoking corner. Everyone there has already given up on life anyway and don't care if they've got their floppy bellies and mahoosive bingo wings out in 100 degrees heat).

The day passed uneventfully – Teenage kids swam from one tropical pool to another, Wifey soaked up the sun's hot rays whilst simultaneously peeking at young blokes through her Ray Bans, and I sulked. Yeah, sulked like a little baby all day simply because I never wanted to come to this sodding water park in the first place and it's cost me a little king's ransom to basically get pissed and burn my moobs.

After 5 hot and angry hours, I was given the nod that wifey had run out of eye candy so we could leave. After doing the "Hop From One Foot To The Other To Avoid The Floorpiss Whilst Knotting Your Pants Round Your Knees" changing room dance, we headed home to the comparative bliss of the Beach Club, aka Mr Disney's Retirement Home For The Monetarily Stupid.

After cooling down in the air-conditioned hotel room, we rounded the day off with a stroll around Epcot. Epcot is the strangest of Mr Disney's Psycho Parks and happened to be right next door to our hotel. Epcot doesn't have the same bawdiness as the other parks and has "The World" as its theme. Different parts of the park represents stuff like "The Land" or "The Sea" and all the way around a huge manmade lake (also full of alligators) there are artificial set pieces of different countries around the world.

The countries all around Epcot are ok. Switzerland's a bit boring but the flag is a big plus.

To me, Epcot is a bit dreary but if it puts your bin's out, you crack on.

Wandering around "The Land" I discovered to my utter dismay that the Captain Eo experience has gone! The one last remaining legacy of Michael Jackson's love for Disney has been cruelly bulldozed. Where else will we be able to see 1980's Michael dressed in leather entertaining the kids, pretending to be a space invader, all in 3D?

Nowhere, that's where. And let's face it, it's for the best.

I reckon somebody must have tipped off Mr Disney about young Michael....

Enjoy Epcot while it lasts dear readers - when Donald Trumpet has done messing the world up, all there will be left at Epcot will be tributes to Humerica and statues of Trumpet himself.

I went to bed REALLY grumpy after a $15.00 gin and tonic, trying to rev myself up for tomorrow's trip to Mr Disney's Secret Lair..... aka The Magic Kingdom.

Grumpy Out

■■■

Day 4 – Mr Disney's Secret Lair (aka The Magic Kingdom)

➢ Calories - 12675 (equivalent to 2 Disney Dining Dollars)
➢ Steps – forgot to set me app, so let's say a round 20,000 for good measure
➢ Number of times I've embarrassed my kids - 37 in one hour (beating my previous record of 35 when I laughed out loud watching Muppets 3D)

Day started Grumpily, as most days do with Wifey and 2 teenage kids crammed into one small room, fighting for the bathroom and smelling of a heady mix of perfume, sweaty feet and trumps.

Despite Teenage Daughter's 17 years, she has never lost that inner toddler ability to spill / smear / wipe all manner of colourful / smelly drinks or food on me. And happily, today was no exception. Halfway to The Lair on the Disney fart bus, she somehow managed to simultaneously bite and throw a Chocolate Peanut Butter Mickey Waffle Brownie Donut Popsicle, right over Grumpy's new white shirt. As you can well imagine, I was not happy about this as it was clean on three days ago. Fear not, as a quick spitwipe from Wifey and a threateningly mumbled "get over yerself, dickhead" sorted me right out and we continued on to The Lair in silence.

As soon as we got in, we came across the Main Street Barber Shop Quartet. These guys are really, really good and we stood and watched them for a few songs. Wifey was well impressed, and why not? Four lean, handsome, talented guys all with beautiful voices, a cheeky grin and a flirty twinkle in their eye. Me, on the other hand, began to wonder if they were **REALLY** barbers. You see, know-it-all Teenage Son "forgot" to get his £4 hair cut before we left Dudley so Wifey had booked him in for a Disney cut at The Beach Club barbers tomorrow.

It was going to cost me $54.00

Yes, $54.00

Fifty four US Dollars.

For a haircut.

By my reckoning, one Disney cut is the equivalent of a whole year's haircuts at Shaky Bobs in Dudley.

Somebody else in the crowd had leaned forwards to put in a request for Camptown Races, so I thought "Why not?" – you don't ask, you don't get.

It must have been my Black Country accent, because he looked at me all blank when I asked him "How much furra quick dry cut aer kid?"

I quickly realised that Wifey and kids had run off in disgust and I eventually caught up with them at Pirates of the Caribbean. We'd Fast Passed it, so we skipped (literally in my case) to the front of the queue, much to the disgust of the hot, bored families standing in line.

"Yo Ho , Yo Ho It's a Pirates Life For Me" was the mantra as we sailed round in our plastic wooden boat, and in no time at all we were shotjust like a pirate cannonball, straight back out into the sunshine. We were just in time for Wifey to watch in adoration / fascination at some pretend Jonny Depp teaching kids how to fight with foam swords in a really bad English accent.

Good looking tosser …..

I eventually managed to get her off him and the stage, and after she'd cooled down, we headed over to Mr Disney's Fantasyland (You know, the one with enchanted houses and castles? You do…, the one where all the set designers must have been on crystal meth?).

First stop - "It's A Small World" - or "It's A Crack House" as Wifey calls it (she doesn't get this ride at all. I **LOVE** it). For those of you that don't know it, it's one of Mr Disney's finest pieces of work, and a real example of what you can achieve with lots of spare cardboard and a twisted imagination. It's a boat ride that wanders through phoney set-pieces, bashed together to represent different countries with little animated people, weird animals and buildings adding their own national flavour. And all the time they sing the most delightful / annoying theme tune.

If you don't know it, go and Google it now.

Go on. I'll wait……

Ready? Good….

Now to the theme tune, repeat after me...

"It's A Crack House after all,
It's A Crack House after all,
It's A Crack House after all,
It's where we all score crack..."

And repeat. And again.

That's your earworm for the day. You're welcome.

It's good to see Mr Disney has updated "It's A Crack House" to reflect the changing political climate in Europe. As you glide towards England, you'll notice that the little British dolls are arguing about Brexit, the Scottish dolls are cleaving a big split in the cardboard and trying to drift off alone and the rest of Europe are lining up opposite England to take our cash and laugh in our faces.

I also noticed that there's a big wall gone up round Mexico and loads of little dolls were being herded into vans by cardboard American police. I wonder what that was about......?

The American part had also had a makeover. Well, I think it was America, it was quite hard to tell. All there is now is a little fat doll in a blonde wig, dancing round a bonfire.

On our way round The Lair we stumbled across a group of grown men playing trombones, dressed up like the soldiers off the Quality Street tin all singing a song about being a friend to Woody that made Wifey cry like a baby. Perfect.

For the rest of the day we staggered from one hot, long queue to the other, bumping into dwarves, princesses, aliens and monsters. In fact, if it hadn't been so hot, we could have been in West Bromwich.

The night ended with all of us watching the incredible fireworks bursting into the night's sky above Mr Disney's Secret Hideout (the Castle). In Grumpy's imagination Mr

Disney lives underneath that big plastic castle thing in the middle, peeking out occasionally to see how many customers he's got....

Halfway through this incredible pyrotechnic display, it made me appreciate why Mr Disney has to charge me $35 for lasagne.

Man alive, how much do those fireworks cost? I get hacked off if I pay more than a pound for a pack of sparklers from Rav's corner shop.

Imagine being Mr Disney, standing watching, scratching your head whilst all of your days takings get puffed up in fairy dust into the Florida sky every night?

"Dang it, Martha, ar guess ar'll jus have to do it awll egen tuhmorra.... ah huk ah huk ah huk..."

On the way back to the fart bus, we stopped off at The Grumpy Shop opposite the Snow White and The Seven Dwarves ride to check my Grumpy merchandise was selling ok (takings are well up since the blog started - I might get a commission from Mr Disney!) then headed home to count what's left of my money.

Fell asleep in a bad mood to weird dreams about Donald Trumpet - yuuuuughhhhhh

Tara a bit,

Grumpy

■■

Day 5 –Water Park Part ii

- ➤ Disney Dining Dollars spent - 24
- ➤ Disney Pluto Pennies spent - 564
- ➤ How many times I have to ask a cast member how the Disney Dining Plan works - 3 times today (a personal record, *curtsies* I thank you)
- ➤ Calories consumed - larger than the GDP of Belgium

The Fam obviously don't think I've suffered enough so off we went again to another bloody water park. They all blur into one mix of sand, screams and disposable nappies to me so we could have been anywhere to be truthful. My guess is we were at Tenalady Drops, but I might be wrong.

After my last experience (see day 3 blog) I was determined to stay covered up this time. So you can imagine my disappointment when I stopped of at the Bibbity Bobbity Surf N Shop Shack on the way in, to find that Disney don't sell a man's burkini.

As we trudged in the Florida sun to find the most uncomfortable red hot plastic beds upon which we would obtain todays third degree burns, the DJ was blasting out "Santa Claus is coming to town"..... you wha? It's 100 degrees, my skin is peeling off and I'm sweating like a West Bromwich teenager with a pregnancy kit.

And why is the sand so hot? Surely with all the money I've handed over so far Mr Disney can afford cold sand? Tight get....

I was already trying to find an excuse to wander off to "find the lockers" (in other words go for several cheeky but welcome expensive beers) when I got dragged off by the teenagers to go on a slide.

A slide. What am I? 8 years old?

I was marched up some god forsaken faux-tropical hill, through warm puddles of kiddy piddle and corn plasters, and forced to choose between Colonic Cyclone or Buttclench Calamity.

There then followed that awkward wait before the teenage life guard can signal that he's considered it safe enough for you to descend (in other words, the green "go" light flicks on his screen), That wait is awful for a chubby middle-aged man. You can't cover yourself up, you can't make conversation for fear of being thought of as a pervert, and you can't make eye contact with anybody under the age of 15 in case they think you're a paedo.

I'm telling you, you don't know how hard it is to be me.....

In the end I chose Buttclench Calamity, only for the reason that the lifeguard / switch flicker attendant was a chubby teenager and had tits bigger than mine. I plopped myself into launch position and when the green light went on I propelled myself forwards down the pipe.

I screamed like a little girl all the way down as the seams between slide pipes ripped in to my muffin tops and my bosoms slapped together, ending in a "spladoosh!" in to the bottom pool similar to that of a launched cruise liner and my butt cheeks on show to a young family cruising by in a dinghy.

I've said it before and I'll say it again.... **why are we doing this to ourselves?** The floors like molten lava, you're finding sand up your arse for days and wasps divebomb your coke. Everywhere is packed with sweaty people and to top it all off you're half naked, exposing your worst wobbly bits to total strangers who you would otherwise ignore in the street.

Eventually The Fam left me alone long enough to do my best Jim Royle impression and I fell into a hot sweaty sleep on the sunbed-cum-grill.

Shortly after, I awoke from a bad dream about being toasted alive by Olaf to find myself being toasted alive whilst listening to the song about Olaf.

I really needed a piddle so quickly dashed to the lazy river (yeah, right like you've never done it) and then after a few more slides (Sphincter Splinter and Nutcrusher Gusher) we had all had enough excitement for one day.

At around 4 o clock, Wifey pricked me to check that I was up to medium rare and when she was satisfied that I had just the right amount of sunburn, she had a little satisfied smile to herself and thankfully allowed us all to leave.

I spent the rest of the evening simultaneously nursing $10 beers and sunburnt muffin tops. And planning for tomorrow's day out..... stay tuned for Grumpy's Adventures in Universal Studios.

Grumpy over and out

■■■■■■■■■■■■■■■■■■■■■■■■■■■■■■■■■■■■■■■

Day 6 – Universal Studios (day one of two)

- ➤ Disney Dining Dollars Balance:

    Scoff Plan x 654 credits
    Quicksilver Meals x 433 credits
    Smiley Waitress "Don't Forget To Tip" Meals x
    254 credits
    (Should be enough to last for the next few
    days)

- ➤ Calorie intake - enough to put an Iron Man
  competitor to shame

This was our Universal Studios mini adventure, so with respect to Mr Universal I'm temporarily changing my name to The Grinch.

Despite the fact that I've already paid for 14 consecutive days unlimited access to Mr Disney's Psychedelic Wonderlands AND to the 14 day, 24 hour all-you-can-stuff-in-your-cakehole Disney Dingo Dollar Dining Plan, Wifey and Teenagers ganged up on me to spend two days at Universal Studios.

I've learnt not to argue.

Despite the fact we've been together for about 20 (???) years and married something like 25, apparently I'm still "in training".

So, like every other married Grinch I do just as I'm told and today we got up at 6 o clock (A.M.) to go and donate more of Grinch's hard-earned cash to the Orlando economy. Like they need it.

Wowzers! What a contrast this place is compared to Disney.

Universal would be Mickey's evil little brother, you know the one that annoys all the family but has done really well for himself? In contrast to Disney, Universal is a bit more "edgy", a bit more coarse and a lot less sanitised. You can't get in unless you've got hair braids, at least two tattoos or one piercing.

And that's just the kids.

If Disney is pop queen Hannah Montana, then Universal would be twerky tattooed Miley Cyrus, if you catch my drift.

Wifey is one of these Harry Potter Mud Blood freaks, so as soon as we arrived we headed straight to Potterland.

Now, I've got nothing against Harry Potter - he's probably a lovely kid and good on him if he's got both magic powers AND can act. Play to your strengths kid, play to your strengths...

I've only ever watched a couple of Harry Potter films - I think they were the early ones before his balls dropped and he got pubic hair. And before Herminey was fit and started to get mildly interesting.

My problem with the Acting Harry Potter is that there was a kid in my class at primary school also called Harry Potter so I'm reminded more of him every time I hear about the films / books / wonky wands / collectible bog roll etc.

Unlike Acting Harry Potter, Schoolkid Harry Potter didn't have any magical powers. Unless of course you count eating plasticine, getting Crayolas stuck up his nose and doing a poo in the sandpit as wizardry. Schoolkid Harry Potter was a real weird kid, always wearing mismatched shoes, a Fray Bentos tin type haircut and always had a distinct smell of spam fritters.

I went around his house once to play, and for a treat his mum gave us Ribena mixed with Lucozade and raspberry ripple ice cream. Thinking about it, Acting Harry Potter is now serving up beer mixed with butter at $10 a throw that tastes the same so maybe it is him after all.....

And they used to drive a blue Ford Anglia.....

And his mum was a bit of a witch.....

Exactamundo! (Is that a Harry Potter spell...?) Maybe it his him after all?

Anyway, I couldn't believe in the magic of Potterland as there's not one single mention of the great magician himself, Paul Daniels. Now there was a magician - anyone who can look like Yoda having a particularly troublesome stiff poo, pull a cracker like Debbie McGhee AND get on prime time TV whilst being shite is a real wizard in my book.

I digress. We went all the way round Potterland and Wifey got her broomstick fixed. As the day wore on, we managed to get around just one of the two massive

Universal parks and did virtually everything we wanted, including my favourite, The Extra Testicular ride.

It's a bit dated now, but ET still brings back loads of fond memories of when my dad got a pirate Betamax video and the entire family crowded into our front room in Dudley to feast on Findus Crispy Pancakes and watch a crackly film through a haze of Benson and Hedges.

The whole family were in floods of tears at that scene where they spot the poor little bugger in that stream, just about to have his knackers bitten off by a raccoon.

And then in the famous scene when the sunflower came back to life signalling ET was still alive, I remember my dad jumping out of his DFS leather armchair, punching the air, spilling his scotch and flicking fag ash all over me grannie.

He was an unlikely hero (ET, not me dad) when you think about it. The world went ET crazy, which was weird considering he looked like a cross between a Krankie and a genital wart.

Anyway, being here in the queue gave me a great excuse to impress Teenage Son and Daughter with a top Grumpy Dad joke.

Dad - "What's E.T short for?"
Bored Teen - "Dunno?"
Dad - "Cos he's only got little legs"

The Extra Testicular ride is a bit weird though and stood next to all these new-fangled 4D "experiences" it now seems absolutely ancient. It appears that ET went a bit off the rails after the film, a bit like another 80's favourite Macaulay Calkin, so you have to help him on a drug run by smuggling him under a blanket with 40 kilos of crystal meth to his junkie friends on Planet Endor. I don't remember him being a druggie in the film... maybe it was in the sequel.

There was too much to see and do across both Universal Psycho Parks in one day, so we saved some stuff to do tomorrow. Stay tuned Grumpy fans.

Bye for now

The Grinch (aka Grumpy)

■■

Day 7 – Universal Studios (day two of two)

- ➢ Calorie count - 33567. Today I've been mostly eating peanut butter and jelly
- ➢ Money spent - lost count. Let's just say I've got Wonga on speed dial
- ➢ Steps - terrible band from the 90's

Having forked out around the same kind of cash for a 2 day park ticket that you would need to buy a 2005 Renault Twingo, day 7 found The Grinch (aka Grumpy) once again in Potterland.

I actually didn't mind so much as I had a sexy "Potter style" dream last night so was secretly hoping that Wifey was going to buy a dressy up Herminey uniform with the long socks. As we went in to one of them wobbly cardboard shops, I discreetly whispered to her if this was a possibility.

"Shurrup, pervert" followed by a swift kick in the shin sorted me right out and no mistake.

Arresto momentum.

So I went outside to sulk, sitting on a baking hot wall wondering exactly how much profit Acting Harry Potter is making on an $10 bottle of "Pumpkin Juice" that's only really dandelion and burdock in a funny shaped bottle.

When Wifey had done buying $50 I-Phone covers, "Magic Spell" books covered in tumble dryer lint and Harry Potter penny chews for the entire population of Dudlaaay at

$5.00 an ounce (it's cheaper to buy them all cocaine), we headed up to the big plastic castle to play Kwidditch. I seem to remember Kwidditch was a game show on daytime BBC with Duncan Norvelle so I was quite looking forward to this. As it turns out, it's another one of these bleeding rides that lasts approximately 1 tenth of the time you queue for it.

Just as we got to the bit at the end of the queue where you entrust you and your family's life with some bored, undertrained teenager strapping you in to a very dangerous moving vehicle, I spotted a sign that said "**Child Swap**".

Oh, I thought, that's a good idea - a sort of trading post a bit like Noel Edmonds 1980's Swap Shop. I wandered in to see if I could swap a 17 year old daughter for a ZX Spectrum or similar, but I don't think they properly understood my Dudlaaay accent.

(I bet some of you male Grumpies are wondering if there's a Wife Swap, eh? Nudge, nudge, knowwarramean...? Well there isn't. And why would there be when you have already found the light of your life? **

** thanks to Wifey for the guest edit

After being violently chucked about in front of a big screen while chasing Acting Harry Potter on a broomstick, we were deposited into the gift shop and one last chance to see if Wifey would buy some Herminey socks.....

Well it was worth asking. If you don't ask, you don't get, right?

When the swelling had gone down we headed over to the new Harry Potter British Railways Train Station that connects the two Universal Psycho Parks. It had only been built in the last few years, so this was our first experience.

Corrr…. Now we're talking. Here's something The Grinch can relate to - good old unreliable British Rail.

Hat's off to Acting Harry Potter, he must have spent a lot of time researching cruddy British Rail train carriages because this one was spot on. The musty smell, the feeling of despair and the scum marks around the window were right on the mark. If he had only got an old tired guy in an ill-fitting uniform selling curled up egg and cress sandwiches, I would have got my trainspotting book out and stayed all day.

We alighted at pretend Kings Cross, and again the attention to detail was amazing. Long queues of unhappy passengers, absolutely no idea when your train is coming or going and to top it off a real life red telephone box with a broken phone, a two inch deep puddle of piss and a wide colourful selection of hooker cards.

Just as we left, Southern Rail set up a flying picket and closed down the station. Some bloke with a cockney accent and a megaphone demanded workers rights for imaginary conductors or at very least a discount on Butterbeer for all his union members. Fair play to Acting Harry Potter, he's nailed it there.

Halfway around the park, 17 year old Teenage Daughter decided she wanted a "hair wrap".

A wha?

I know I'm old and grumpy but surely this must be one of the most stoopid fashion ideas. You actually <u>pay</u> someone to get a chunk of your hair and wrap it in string.

That's it. That's all it is.

$3.00 an inch.

To look like you've got string in your hair.

I don't get it.

And I'll tell you what else I don't get - the fascination with eyelashes and eyebrows. When did it become fashionable to look like you have two slugs above your eyes and eyelashes the size of a pantomime cow?

When did it become attractive to look like you've just been scared by a ghost?

I can just imagine the conversation at the West Bromwich "*On The Lash* Brow Bar"

"Oroight Britnaay, wotch yow havin terday?"

"Ar dough kno Chelsaaaay…. Ar cor deside between *Frozen Shock* or *Quizzical Pantomime Dame*"

$30,00 later (or ten inches) we were off to The Hulk roller coaster and finally something that looks expensive so I can get my money's worth.

Essentially, The Hulk roller coaster is a big, green mechanical squiggle in the sky. It looks like a toddlers bored doodle that his hipster designer dad has seen after a night on the bong and thought "thatsh a gud idea.....I can build that!"

The Hulk roller coaster utterly defies logic while your body defies gravity. These rides are perfect if you have always had some weird ambition to feel your ball bag tickling the top of your own neck, or take a real good close up look at your own sphincter.

(Grumpy's top tip - before your next roller coaster trip, grab a handful of big, long nuts and bolts from B & Q. Go on any roller coaster as a single rider so you can get next to a total stranger. Just as you get to the end of the first steep clanky bit, casually drop a handful of aforementioned nuts and bolts on the floor and look immediately at their safety harness and say "blimey I hope THAT'S not important.....")

Our Universal trip finished a little earlier due to the torrential rain and we were forced to take cover under a deserted concession stand. Teenage Son had one job, to remember the $10 Disney ponchos. Like the fab Teenage Son he is, and like they all are, he immediately forgot them as soon as we left our hotel room, so Wifey used her magical womanly powers to make some out of Universal bin liners. Turns out they're better and thicker than real ones....

Wifey got carried away with her new-found skill of scratting in bins and pretty soon started to offer them out to random passers-by. Eventually, Teenage kids stopped her just at the point where she was trying to sell them and we all made a dash to the exit, resplendent in our Binbag Ponchos (went to school with him - lovely Mexican lad)

Ended the day drinking expensive beers and applying for the second and third job I now need to pay for all this mularkey.

Over and out, The Grinch

■■■ ■ ■

Day 8 – Laundry Day

> ➤ Step count – 5765 / Drunken Shuffle count – 42316
> ➤ Calories consumed - 6754 (1 x Mickeys Buttermilk Fried Chicken n Syrup Waffle Burger. And Fries. And slaw)
> ➤ Arguments with teenagers about Fast Passes - 5 (lost 4, drawn 1)

The one holiday day us Grumpies hate - ... ** shudders ** ...... Laundry Day

Ladies, **WE** know that **YOU** know that all men are stupid. That's a known fact passed down from loving mother to daughter since time began. But ladies, never underestimate the special relationship between men and stupidity as it just keeps on giving (For example, simply Google "Donald Trump")

I for one can vouch for almost a lifetime of stupidity ranging from inconsequential acts of mild buffoonery to wardrobe collapsing, car crashing, marriage threatening idiocy.

Ladies, please don't pity us. It's as much in our DNA as the gene that makes your nostril hair grow an inch a day as soon as you hit 40. Every boy and man has within him this invisible super power and there's nothing we can do to stop it.

No matter how big, strong, powerful or good looking, every man is only ever one neuron away from doing or saying something stupid, like wearing a flowery shirt, putting something on his head, swinging his willy from side to side or starting a war.

Some men try. They recognise their own and the faults of their brothers and spend a lifetime trying double hard not to let the stupid leak out. Men in this category tend to be trendy gay guys, vicars, your wife's secret crush and George Clooney.

They do have a place in society but quite frankly are letting the side down and should not be trusted by any other man.

To demonstrate my own (in)ability, today I did something double stupid - I took another woman's laundry out of the washing machine......

Oooooooohhhhhh. O. Ooo......

(Wow..... is it me or has it just gone really cold in here, lads?)

How are us Grumpies supposed to know the etiquette of The Laundry?

I genuinely thought I was helping out.....

I should have guessed that the laundry room was no place for me the first time when I went last week with Wifey. 7.00 am on the dot, a slow but glorious procession of Holiday Mums headed down to The Beach Club laundry room, all hunched up with big straggly bags containing a weeks' worth of dribble stained t shirts, smelly socks and pants with skidmarks that would make Lightning McQueen proud.

In its own way, this is something quite beautiful to behold. The sight of these earthy women, all plodding together in line with the mutual feminine goal of washing poo out of underpants. It almost warrants its own background music to be piped through the designer bushes as Holiday Mums sashay towards Disney's Watering Hole to beat dirty clothes against a stone. (If you're reading Mr Disney, I want royalties if you turn this into a film).

Earlier in the holiday, I was Wifey's laundry Sherpa so I dutifully walked behind her carrying the bags down to The Laundry. As soon as we entered the laundry room, her whole being changed - she turned in to some mad female Inspector Gadget and simultaneously did things to washing machines that I don't understand and used folding techniques that were half body popping / half magic trick.

It truly was a sight to behold – I seriously thought of getting her a spot on Britain's Got Talent.

The end result was an immaculate pile of fresh, beautifully fragranced clothes ready to be spoiled again in a matter of hours.

So, can you imagine my fear when she told me I'd got to do this on my own? She's a Black Belt on Candy Crush and was stuck on a new level, so I was given the simple task of going ahead and getting the laundry started.

Hence how I got in to trouble.

Now, here's a Grumpy confession.... I don't understand women - they all completely baffle me. I don't read the subtle signals given out, be it good or bad. I don't get the mood swings until it's too late.

And I really can't follow the changes of mind. That's a doosey.....

And while I'm at it and feeling brave hiding behind my book, I don't understand bras.

God, I love bras. But why make them so deliciously, fabulously attractive with thin lace and just enough support..... then so bloody hard to get off? Why not make it easy for fumbley fingered blokes like me, like fitting a simple button or just use Velcro?

Now I've given an indication just how much women scare / baffle me, I enter the laundry timid and alone to be confronted by two Holiday Mums working away in silence, patiently folding their freshly laundered washing into neat piles, ready to be re-soiled almost immediately by the rest of the ungrateful family.

Neither looked at me.

Do I say hello? Engage in conversation? Smile?

On one hand I don't want to be ignorant, on the other I don't want them to think I'm either flirting or a pervert. One smile could either end up with me being bashed over the head Dick Emery style or with them ganging up on me and starting a protest march round Epcot.

In the end it didn't matter as pretty soon they left in dignified silence and elegantly drifted off as if mysteriously called away by Ariel, The High Priestess of

Laundry (If Mr Disney does make this into a film, I'd like Nigella Lawson to play that part)

So I'm all alone and safe in the laundry and it so happens that a washing machine has just stopped…..

But no-one comes to empty it's hot, steamy contents.

So I wait.
And wait.
And wait.

After 15 minutes I begin to panic as I've got Fast Passes for "It's A Crack House" (see blog Day 4 readers) so I start to think I should just take the stuff out. I look nervously out of the door to see if anyone's coming.

No-one in sight.

So quick as a flash I grabbed my opportunity, swiftly opening the machine door and grabbing a handful of washing to put on the big folding table.

Oh, I forgot to add earlier that women also freak me out when they seemingly appear out of nowhere, silently like a stalking tiger…… this usually happens when you're looking at something naughty on your phone, or checking out pictures of your ex-girlfriend on your laptop.

As was the case now.

I didn't even hear the door open behind me. Nor the Holiday Mum sashay into the room. But I <u>did</u> hear her say:

"**Excuuusse me**…..? Do you mind?"

I let out a pathetic yelp and turned around to explain, plead forgiveness or just throw myself at her feet sobbing and confess my lifetime of male stoopidity when I realised that I was holding two big handfuls of spotty knickers, a huge pair of Spanx and a frilly but functional bra.

And that's when Wifey walked in.

In a feminine millisecond, Wifey surveyed the scene, took stock and totally understood the situation.

She could have looked at the farce in front of her eyes and realised her husband had made an obvious mistake, rolled her eyes and apologised in a "ha ha, isn't he an idiot!" kinda way.

She could have even been a bit fighty, a quality my scarred chin knows she possesses, and defended her brave, handsome husband who was merely being chivalrous by helping out.

Alas no, the feminine intuition kicked in and she very quickly realised that the pathetic scene in front of her was simply that her bumbling idiot husband had been caught going through another woman's briefs, and she sided with Holiday Mum.

Suffice to say that the two women bonded immediately over my obvious male stupidity and laughed it off together in a secret language, walking away arm in arm at the elbow and eventually becoming friends on Facebook.

I, on the other hand, spent the rest of the day cowering like a puppy who's just piddled on the new carpet.

To make up for my stupidity, I booked a "Smiley Waitress Don't Forget To Tip" Meal at the posh restaurant in Animal Kingdom Lodge (2 Disney Dingo Dollars each needed for this one, Grumpies. No expense spared)

I love it at Animal Kingdom Lodge. We stayed there on our first ever trip a few years ago when the kids were little and still thought I was a cool dad. I love all the animal stuff, and especially how the hotel staff randomly choose a toddler to feed to the tigers each night.

I'm only joking...

It's every other night.

We ate in a restaurant with a spectacular view over the faux Serengeti plains. I got totally the wrong idea - I thought it was like a fish restaurant where you choose which one you want. I really liked the look of a chunky looking antelope, but Smiley Waitress was having none of it.

I was forced to choose from the menu and if you're like me, you know it's going to be too posh when you can't understand half of it.

And I bet it's gonna come on a slate...... When was that made a thing and who's stupid idea was it? I bet you that Heston Bloomingtarl started it. Why would anyone want to eat food off building materials? What's next - mash on a plank? Stew on a brick?

And another thing - when did it become compulsory to "pull" meat? You can't buy any meat now without it being pulled, shredded and steeped in greasy BBQ sauce. Can't I just have meat?

Mind you, pulled pudding is a lovely way to finish a meal.

Anyway, I couldn't choose as the venison was a little dear but they did have ox tongue. Only problem with tongue is you never know when you've stopped eating it.

In the end, I played safe and had the British Empire Stack - a Pulled Dodo Burger with Duck Billed Platypus Mash, topped off with White Rhino Horn Shavings in a Stewed Panda jus. Delish.

Then off to bed to burp and trump and annoy the teenagers.

That's all folks

Grumpy

■■

Day 9 (I think... they're all beginning to blur into one) – Double Park Day

> ➤ Regrets - I've had a few
> ➤ Disney Dingo Dollars left - enough to feed school dinners to a moderately sized comprehensive for a week
> ➤ Steps - who cares?

Bless all my fellow bloggers but what's the obsession with counting how many steps you've taken? What's the point?

Why not count blinks? Burps? Twitches?

Grumpy dads should have a Fartometer (by the time you've finished reading this Mr Disney will have designed and patented that. I know he's reading my blogs)

Hello Mr Disney, loving your work!!

To be honest I did fall for the steps thing at the beginning of the holiday, but it became too much competition with The Fam so I gave up (and because I kept losing). It was getting ridiculous - if Wifey hadn't "got me steps up" at the end of each day, she'd mince up and down the corridors late at night in The Beach Club like some drug crazed athlete training for the marathon walk at the Olympics.

In the end, I secretly strapped my FitBit to the back of the guy next door's mobility scooter overnight and took his shock absorbers out. Big win for Grumpy that day, Fam (674,652 steps before his axle broke)

For today's kicks, The Fam decided we needed to push the limits of our physical and mental endurance by doing **TWO** of Mr Disney's Psychedelic Wonderlands **ON THE SAME** day. I don't think they have made me suffer enough.

I've already decided my next holiday is going to be far more relaxing, so I've booked a fortnight living in a Peruvian jungle with that Bear Grills, fending off scorpions and drinking my own widdle (there is an optional upgrade for a daily scrotum grate and sleeping with your head in a box of moths so I'm saving up for that)

My nosey Teenage Daughter "overheard" a cheeky tipoff in the Beach Club jacuzzi about how to get a Pandora Bracelet Avatar Ride Fast Pass. A Fast Pass for the Avatar ride is like a Willy Wonka Golden Ticket. In the build up to this holiday, all the talk on It's Orlando Time was how amazeballs this ride was, but how difficult it was to get on it due to the massive queues.

So imagine our delight when Teenage daughter's nosey tip off came good…..

Apparently, Mr Disney releases a new batch of Fast Passes for all the popular rides each day, based on the demand, park numbers, previous day's takings etc. He does this at precisely 10.37 AM (Eastern US time) and if you can manage to tap your way quick enough on the Disney App, you're in with a chance.

And that's how we got our Fast Pass – at 10.36 on the dot, we were all in the hotel room together, sitting in silent anticipation as Wifey held the phone at the ready (she's got the quickest, nimblest fingers so she had the tappy task)

10.37! Bang on time, a window opened up on the App like a secret cave entrance and in a blur of tappy fingers we were in!

You have no choice with the time slot you're given, and ours was only in a few hours' time so after bags were made ready, hair was "up in bobbles" and sun tan cream applied, off we trotted to catch a Mr Disney fart powered bus to the Animal Kingdom to see what the fuss is all about.

** takes his Grumpy hat off **

IT'S AWESOME!!!!

YOU GET TO RIDE ON A BANSHEE THROUGH PANDORA LIKE IN THE FILM!!!

BEST RIDE EVER!!

LOVED IT!!

IT MADE ME HAPPY!!

** puts Grumpy hat back on **

As all good rides do, our banshee kindly dropped us off in the Pandora gift shop (luckily no cheap bracelets in sight). But Grumpy did spot a very interesting sign...... "Become An Avatar!"

For just $74.99 (plus tax, Grumpies LOVE the extra hidden tax, eh?) you can turn a real human into an Avatar like they did to Sigourney Weaver in the film.

Now I know they look like a junky Smurf on steroids, but I confess that I do find Avatar (women) weirdly attractive. The slim muscular legs, athletic build, the long arms with the extra reach that could get right in to the back of the deep freeze....

So, with this in mind I discreetly asked if they had the technology to "Avatar" Wifey and in no time at all she was being biometrically measured up by a teenage scientist in an ill-fitting uniform called Chad.

I was getting all excited at the thought of it! Imagine if she could attach herself to one of those banshees? Providing we could find one in Dudley, of course.

She could fly me anywhere! Think of the money I'd save on petrol! And it would be a doddle cleaning the gutters out.

To my perverted and financial dismay, I soon realised that I wasn't getting a life size Wifey Avatar, but a plastic 8 inch replica doll that looked a bit like Wifey if she pressed her face hard up against a window. Fair play to Chad the teenage scientist though - he programmed the Wifey Avatar to quickly develop the same Wifey characteristics and mannerisms and in no time it had perfected the arms crossed tutting look of disapproval and had stopped me in my tracks to scoop some flaky wax out of my ear in public.

I was frog marched back over to Pretend Asia as the Disney App said there was no queue for the Himalayan

Everest ride, so after a quick up and down and round and round looking for the Yeti (still no sign of him) we trudged back to get Mr Disney's Fart Bus to start part two of the Iron Man challenge.

Hi Ho, Hi Ho, off to Hollywood Studios we go......

We arrived just in time for it to absolutely chuck it down. And I mean chuck it down. Orlando rain is amazing – one minute it's bone dry and red hot, the next minute a massive bluey grey cloud appears from nowhere and in the time it takes you to say:

"Oooh, look love, it might rai....." It's raining.

Big dollops of rain. Relentless, angry fat rain that immediately soaks you right though to your pants before you get chance to wrestle with your $10.00 Mr Disney binbag poncho.

Then, just as it started and looks like it's in for the day, it stops and the sun comes out. Within minutes, the sky is clear blue again and everything is back to bone dry.

I think Orlando weather is bi-polar.

Luckily, we found something indoors that helped us avoid the worst of the rain, and as it turns out we may have stumbled upon something you may have all missed. It's something that hasn't had a great deal of publicity and certainly hasn't resulted in collectible toothbrushes, dolls and duvet covers...

I'll share a secret with you. Mr Disney has made a film about two sisters who fall out. It's based in Iceland and I didn't quite catch the name, but I *think* it's called "It's Sodding Freezing".

Anyway, in order to brainwash all the kids before it gets released, Mr Disney has very kindly built a big theatre at Hollywood Studios where all Disney guests are marched in and forced to learn the words to the songs. I have to say, they are very catchy and I was thoroughly captivated.

Trust me on this - It's going to be a big hit. I think I went on about it too much afterwards over dinner, and in the end Wifey snapped "Let It Go!"

Our last appointment on the two park day was with yet more food as we had only had 6000 calories each. So in order to complete our Mr Disney Eating Challenge for the day, we had the most enormous Italian meal.

You ever had that feeling when you eat too much and you start to hallucinate? That's pretty much every day in Disney.

At dessert (which we always have as it's included in the price - I'm from the Black Country so you get your money's worth) the fam ordered Key Lime Pie, Chocolate Cheesecake and Ice Cream. I asked for a stomach pump and a gym membership.

Back home to The Beach Club / Mr Disney's Rest Home for an erotic dream about Avatars.

See you tomorrow for another rant

Grumpy, done

∎∎

Day 10 – Sodding Shopping

- ➢ Steps - 5632
- ➢ Tiptoes - 456 (to leave the room to secretly watch Game of Thrones)
- ➢ Number of "Can we take it to go?" puddings in Mr Disney's Beach Club bedroom fridge - 8

10 sleeps for 4 people in one hotel room is beginning to take it's toll my Grumpy friends. There's not a spare bit of space on the bedroom floor that isn't taken up by knickers, expensive trainers, rucksacks or Disney carrier bags ("they'll make lovely presents") filled with tat for kids I either don't know or like. It's like we've turned into one of them hoarders, you know the freaks they have on Channel 4 that haven't had a bath since Ant and Dec were PJ and Duncan?

I half expected to come back to the room to find that nice girl off Obsessive Compulsive Cleaners wearing a white forensic suit and marigolds, doing a swab test on the fridge and dry vomiting at the sight of Teenage Son's underpants.

And the smell... it shouldn't be a surprise really considering we're on Mr Disney's SupercalorificXLstodgyhalitosis Eating Plan. When the lights go out at night in our room it's like the frog chorus.

So, we left the room to be deep cleaned and fumigated and headed over to a place Wifey had banged on about called Disney Springs.

Finally! A relaxing day at a posh Disney Spa to soothe old Grumpy's tired bones and some long overdue "me time".

Readers, I was duped....

Disney Springs is not a health spa where smiley, Diana Dors type bosomy women rub special Asian oils into your temple but.....

I can hardly say it..... a shopping centre!!!!

Noooooooooooooo.........

As you may have already read, I don't understand women and don't get shopping. Please excuse my stupidity for asking, but...

Why do you always need such a big Mary Poppins style handbag and what in God's name is in it? And why is it so important to ALWAYS have it with you….?

Why do you take your purse out if you've got no money? Wifey actually phoned me once from nipping / popping out to Tesco to ask me "do you want anything cos I've got no money...."

Why does it seem that you take back MORE to the shops than you actually bought? Each Wifey pop to our local shopping centre results in three more trips to take back the stuff she bought and didn't like.

Why do you all have to have "straight" hair? What's wrong with bent hair?

And while I'm asking, what's the difference between grips, bobbles, bands and clips? And why are you always running out of them? Why don't you carry more in them big mysterious handbags?

Grumpies don't do shopping unless it involves alcohol, Ford Cortina engine parts or a new shed. The best bit about this shopping was that the fam don't mind me buggering off to be Grumpy on my own. But after a few beers I was curious to see why so many happy women had loads of big expensive looking bags with their own Grumpies shuffling behind looking shell shocked, so off I toddled to check the prices of the tat in Mr Disney's shops.

You never know, I might find a starter motor for a Ford Cortina.

My god you can buy Disney everything! And at only an extra 250% more 'cos it's got Disney on it!

After half an hour of retail madness I was just getting fed up of looking at Disney towels, Disney clocks, Disney pyjamas, Disney bloody everything when I spotted Disney Pharmacy so off I popped to have a look.

Wow, what a great store that is! I spent ages looking up and down the aisles, fascinated by all the incredible merchandise on offer. There was so much choice.

I couldn't decide between Mickey and Minnie's Anal Bleaching Kit or The Donald Duck Home Colonic Irrigation, so in the end I played safe and went for 25 kilos of Goofy's Teeth Whitening Paste (although at my age I was tempted by The Disney Erectile Dysfunction pills, ironically sponsored by Pinocchio)

Happy with my purchase, I met up with The Fam for the next instalment of the Mr Disney Shove It All Down Eating Challenge as we hadn't had anything for 2 whole hours.

We slurped and munched away on BBQ ribs as Wifey told me how much money she'd saved me whilst simultaneously spending all of my money.

Now at this point, let me introduce you to Molly.

Molly is a 10 month old cockapoo that is as cute as a button and has become the centre of The Fam's world. I was just thinking about Molly as the last of my spending money was being wasted on Disney tat, only because when I get back I've also got to pay the dodgy bloke next door on benefits £35 a day for Molly to sleep in his front room, eat Bonios and sniff his other dog's bums.

Don't get me wrong, I like Molly but nowhere near as much as the rest of The Fam. As Molly bounded happily into our household, she simultaneously pushed me down a place in the Wifey pecking order as follows:

1 Kids
2 House
3 Molly
4 Candy Crush
5 Full tank of petrol
6 Husband

I'm telling you this for good reason - as we built up a stack of bones that would look at home pushed to the side of an archaeological dig, I happened to say:

"Molly would love them bones. I wonder what she's doing now"

Judging by the awkward silence, the sniffles and then the sobbing, I now know it wasn't a good thing to say.....

So The Fam didn't speak to me for some time and instead talked about how much they missed a dog that doesn't even know we've gone and is probably having a whale of a time dragging its bum on Mr Bradfords' lino.

When we got back to Mr Disney's Home For The Dollar Demented, the leftover puddings in the fridge had turned and the maid had refused to clean the room until she could see the floor.

Perfect end to another Grumpy day in paradise.

Grumpy out

■■

Day 11 – Disco Cove

> ➤ Step - 1,2,3,4,5,6,7,8 ....and Kick... 2,3,4,5,6,7,8
> ➤ Number of times I've asked Wifey if we can go to Hooters - 15
> ➤ Number of times we've been to Hooters - 0

I always wake up before The Fam so this morning I pulled my shorts on over my jama bottoms, popped my baseball cap on headed on down to the Disney shop / café to complete my daily chores. These include topping up the free refills, snaffling tea bags and nicking all the free tubs of peanut butter - 25 in one day is my record (as mentioned, I am from The Black Country and my nan would turn in her grave if I "day get me munnys wuth").

I mention the Black Country a lot, so here's' a Quick Black Country joke for ya (Breathe in deeply and channel your inner Noddy Holder - you've all got one)

"Wot's the diffrunce between a buffalo and a bison?

Yo cor wash yer faerce in a buffalo"

By the way, this very special day happened to be my birthday.

I knew The Fam had a birthday surprise in store as I caught a glimpse of Teenage daughter's laminated Disney itinerary (bless her, she loves a plan) and I saw the words *Disco Cove*. Great! A bit of the old D-I-S-C-O will be perfect on Grumpy's birthday - you can't beat Luther Vandross to get 'ol snake hips throwing a few shapes.

Alas no. Disco in this instance is short for "Discovery" and the Cove bit is.... well, it's a cove.

Basically, I'm spending my birthday in a posh water park. Now if you've read my previous blogs (and why wouldn't you? They're hilarious!) you may know that I'm no good at water parks for many varying reasons.

I've thought about it since and I reckon I developed an aversion to stepping on wet floors having been scarred for life after swimming lessons when I was a kid at Dudley baths. To get to the pool you had to wade through a sheep dip thing containing the most lethal mix of plasters, pubic hair and 1970's chemicals (this was when they were still testing stuff by dropping it in rabbits' eyes).

Once, a kid in front of me slipped over in it and by the time they pulled him out he looked like something out of Planet of the Apes.

Turns out that Disco Cove is a cross between a private beach club and an aquarium, with the added excitement provided by dolphin swims and a tank full of sharks. Yes, you heard me right, sharks.

You can actually pay to swim with sharks......

The day didn't start well for me when we were fitted for wetsuits. The Fam were kitted out in no time but when he took a look at me he realised he'd have to go into the "special room" for "the big fella".

Smarmy Git.

Wifey doesn't do water and she definitely does <u>not</u> do fish. Or dolphins. Even as we walked across the beach to our sunbeds, she was convinced the dolphins in the lagoon were trying to get her ("if one of them dolphins comes near me I'll punch it in the blowhole")

Wifey finds a sunbed conveniently next to the blondest, most handsomest lifeguard well away from Flipper and shoos me and the kids on our way.

"Go and enjoy yourself" she says as she slowly strips off and oils herself up whilst staring at Chip or Biff as he pretends to keep lookout on that big tennis umpire chair (we all know you're just gawping at girls behind those shades...... jammy get)

The upshot is that I get to spend my birthday in a tight, red hot wetsuit, dressed like sharkbait, tippytoeing on the baking sand and swimming in a big fishpond with hundreds of excitable kids piddling in the water while the fish eat their eczema.

Happy Birthday Me.

While I was snorkelling in the big Disco Cove fishpond, I overheard a little girl say "mummy, mummy I want to swim with the whales...". Cheeky little bugger wasn't smiling five minutes later when I accidentally trod on her Frozen sandcastle.

After an all you can scoff lunch and a quick power nap, I waddled quickly back to the water (I needed a wee and the toilets were miles away). I had finally got the hang of the snorkelling lark so after a few laps of the fishpond I swam majestically over to where they keep the sharks.

The shark tank is actually **inside** the fishpond, separated only by a glass wall.

As I got close, I swear the sharks got all lively and started nudging each other. I never even knew a shark could lick it's lips. It was almost like they'd picked up a scent of blubber, a bit like that old Bisto advert with Linda Bellingham.

I was getting all cocky, lobbing the V's at them as they tried to bite through the glass when I looked behind me and saw this big black fin...... I screamed through my snorkel and a little bit of poo came out of my bum. Just as I started to do an impression of that girl that gets killed in the first scene of Jaws, I flung myself around to discover it was my own flipper...

I gathered up Teenagers and returned to the sunbeds just in time to see Wifey pretend to drown so she could get mouth to mouth from Chip. We ushered her protesting and throwing more water on herself into a taxi and headed back to Mr Disney's Rest Home For The Financially Destitute.

Just time for a quick change and remove all remaining sand from every orifice before shooting out for a birthday Chinese meal in Epcot (ni hao to any Chinese readers!) Grumpy Fact - I can actually speak a little Chinese having spent some time over there working.

Go Me Uh

Which as it happens was the name of the waiter who showed us to our table for another 10,000 calorie meal including something so deeply fried CSI Disney wouldn't have identified it.

Bang on nine o clock Mr Disney even put on a firework display for me, which was nice of him, but I'd rather have had the money.

There was just time for one last desperate request to Wifey for a nightcap at Hooters, and after the bruising had gone down, sulked off to bed.

Over and out, Grumpy

■■■

Day 12 – Bush Gardens

- ➢ Disney Dining Dollars balance - still enough to eat all day every day til Christmas. Next year.
- ➢ Money spent - greater than the cost of my first 5 cars combined
- ➢ Calories - moving in to the area when one has to consider a gastric band.

Does anyone else having funny dreams when you're on holiday? I woke startled this morning after dreaming I was helping Jon Snow and Rick Wakeman move house. We were helped by a giant kangaroo who had moussaka round his face and cat who was laughing and taking pictures while being chased by a giant Mickey Waffle. I reckon Mr Disney's putting some mind-bending chemicals into them free refills.

Had a bit of a lie in and watched some American TV.

Wowzer! Is there a haemorrhoid epidemic here that I've missed? Every 5 minutes there's an advert for some soothing ointment called Anuslube or Rectaleaze:

"Do you suffer with bum grapes? Tagnuts getting you down? Then try this, new improved Sphinctasalve!"

And every other advert is for a cure for a medical condition, where the disclaimer at the end states it MAY cause the medical condition it's trying to cure! Or... DEATH! Who's going to buy that?

Imagine going into the Disney Pharmacy and asking "you got any smallpox mate? Oh and a small tub of scurvy while you're there..."

So for today's challenge on this eating and marching holiday, we're going 100 miles away to visit a worse Psychedelic Wonderland than the 4 I've already paid for. I did get slightly interested when I heard Wifey say we were going to "Bush Gardens".... a misunderstanding which led to me having to quickly delete my browser history.

Mr Disney doesn't do a fart bus to Tampa so we hired a brand new car from Alamo (cowboys) with only 120,000 miles on the clock. Driving in America gives me an excuse to listen to my favourite type of music - country and western.

Aah there's nothing better for Grumpy than some good old miserable tunes about yer gal running off with your best friend or being mangled by John Deere Tractor.

I think Conway Twitty said it best with his big hit " I Don't Know Whether To Kill Myself Or Go Bowling" or was it Kenny Rogers' " When You Leave Walk Out Backwards, So I'll Think You're Walking In"?

Wifey likes the more religious ones like "Drop Kick Me, Jesus, Through The Goalposts Of Life" by Jonny Cash.

Here's Grumpy's top 3 country and western hits:

1. "Get Your Biscuits In The Oven And Your Buns In The Bed"

2. "Her Teeth Were Stained, But Her Heart Was Pure"
3. " If She Puts Lipstick On My Dipstick I'll Fall In Love"

We reached Bush Gardens just as the whole fam launched into the chorus of "Mama Get The Hammer (There's A Fly On Papa's Head)". Top stuff.

Bush Gardens was hot and empty. Eerily empty. I've never been inside an empty fun park, and this was strange……

It could have been the set where they did the big reveal in Scooby Doo, you know the one where they unmask the local Jimmy Saville who's been haunting the fairground? To be fair, I wouldn't be here myself if it wasn't for my pesky kids.

Bush Gardens is a mix of bonkers roller coasters, bored, caged up animals and petting zoos. In the middle of the park, there's a wild animal safari which is surrounded by the compulsory steam railway, and there's gift shops selling tat EVERYWHERE. I imagine it's great when it's a little busier, but to be here when there's hardly a soul in the place was just a bit too weird.

We ambled around in the boiling heat, stopping off to look at bored pheasants, gawp at flamingos on one leg and get up close with the parrots in the bird enclosure. For a couple of dollars, you can buy a pot of bird food that guarantees the birds will swoop down and attack / shit on you. For a few moments, we all stood with hands outstretched waiting for a bird to use us as a perch or a pooing post. It must have been my aftershave as no birds would come near me (story of my life) However, one lucky girl had TWO parrots on her - she must have been an expert cos she looked like she'd had a cockatoo.

The reason we were here is because Teenage Son and Daughter love roller coasters. I'm usually ok with them but the teenagers working the rides here are the ones that must have failed the interview with Mr Disney. They were all a lot less smiley and a lot more scruffy.

One spotty kid organising the queue on Rectal Blast (or Vomit Comet, can't remember exactly) had an ill-favoured look about him. He was a bit cock-eyed and set me on edge - if he had 3 more chromosomes he could have been a pork pie. He also had an uneasy interest in my crotch as he strapped me in really tight – and as soon as the ride shot off I found out why. The force used to propel you upwards into the Florida sky also pins part of your body into the seat. The seat was one of those designs where your legs are either side of a central support, meaning that as soon as G force pushes your crotch hard against the divide, your ballbag gets splayed in two then bumped up and down for the next thirty seconds. When we eventually got back to the station, my scrotum was splayed across my upper thighs in the shape of a flying fox and as the kid retrieved my harness, he had a worryingly pervy look on his face…..

Luckily, we survived this and many more crazy rides and lived to spend another day. By 4 o clock, the thunderstorms were threatening to roll over once more, so we trudged out of the park in the 100 degree heat, feet hurting and crotch wetter than an otters' pocket.

Mr Bush has a nice park with lots of great rides and probably more smelly animals than Animal Kingdom, but its a win for Mr Disney from Grumpy. I don't think you can trust a park owner when he has to invent his own mascots, like Walter The Weasle or a Arry The Aadvark. And it's nothing to do with the fact that I've had to pay for my own food and drink today instead of using up any of my Disney Dingo Dollars......nothing at all. Honest.

Back to the car lot and luckily Alamos' "brand new" rental car hadn't collapsed into a heap of steamy metal with the tyres skewiffed on all four sides, and in no time, we're back on the I-4 setting course for Mr Disney's Old Folks Home Resort. Jimmy Buffet had just started his All Time Country Love Songs Show so we were treated to hits like " I Knew I'd Hit Rock Bottom When I Woke Up On Top Of You" and "I Hate Every Bone In Your Body Except Mine".

We reached Disney just as the thunderstorms eventually did roll in. There's supposed to be a hurricane here this week - It's ok by me as I've been secretly stocking up on Mickey Waffles. If we don't eat them I'm taking them back as my shed needs propping up.

We had dinner in the French bit of Epcot (we would have eaten Mexican but there was American border guards in place) and fair play to Mr Disney as he's not only managed to capture the very essence of French cuisine by charging me $30.00 for stewing steak and burnt chips but he's also been able to find the rudest most obnoxious waiters too! Man, I love France and I love French culture but mon dieu they know how to be rude to paying guests.

Tres bien Monsieur Disnee!

Back to the room to check my bank balance and fell asleep crying into my pillow.

Perfect

Grumpy out

■■■

Day 13 –Magic Kingdom and MNSSHN

- ➢ Disney Dingo Dollar Balance - enough left to survive Hurricane Irma
- ➢ Pounds gained - 12
- ➢ Pounds lost - almost all of mine to Mr Disney at a poxy exchange rate of $1.27. Pffft

This is our last full day in Disney, so the fam were determined to get the best out of it. Equally, I was determined to get my money's worth out of Mr Disney's Roll Up, Roll Up, Scoff Till You Drop Dingo Dollar Dining Plan.

So while the fam sunbathed, gymmed and crushed candy, I wandered from one refill station to another cramming Mr Disney's plastic mug with as much dandelion and burdock (I refuse to call it root beer) as I could drink and adding to my stash of ranch dressing and peanut butter. I drank so much I must have looked like a guy lost in the desert who finally found a water hole. Well, if desert water holes had a wide choice of sugary drinks, ice, straws and a selection of condiments (slightly reduced availability this day as I'd gone down in my big cargo shorts with the extra-large pockets).

After I came down from the sugar rush I joined the fam for some sun. We all take extra care in the sun - Wifey and the kids slap on factor 30 to keep them safe. I burn easy, so I pop on a deep sea divers suit and balaclava. I'm no good at sun cream - I either miss bits and burn to a crisp or put too much on and look like I've glazed myself like a human Chelsea Bun.

Sometimes, if I'm just sunbathing in a t-shirt, I'll get the suntan cream so wrong it looks like I've come to perform a French mime.

And I don't do headphones.

Headphones neither fit or suit me. If I wear a pair of Beats I look like a 1960's Russian cosmonaut about to be launched in to space in a dangerous looking rocket with just some weird oddly humanlike monkey as company. And if I use the "in ear" type ones there is not a minute that they actually fit properly. If they do stay in any slight movement of my head results in one or both of them popping out. Sometimes I only have to blink and both plugs pop out like corks.

So after about 15 minutes in the sun wiping sweaty sun cream out of my eyes and fighting earplug wires I've had enough so go for a wander around Mr Disney's Marketplace shop. I was hoping to be able to swap my remaining Disney Dingo Dollars for something useful. Never one to miss an opportunity, I see he'd stocked up on Goofy's Hurricane Irma Survival Shelter and Pluto's Tastes Great Like Momma Used To Make Dried Grits. Top stuff, Mr Disney.

The smiley assistant wouldn't let me swap 50 credits for a 6 pack of Budweiser beer so I sulked back to the room to get ready for this afternoon's trip to Mr Disney's Secret Lair.....

As I said, it's our last Disney day so the fam wanted to do all the stuff we hadn't seen yet. Using Grumpy's Translator (only $86.99 + tax from all Mr Disney's shops) this actually means more walking, more queuing, more spending and less time drinking expensive beer.

Anyroad, in we go and after a trip to Tomorrowland (I really hope that's not what my Tomorrow looks like) it just so happened that we got to the front of the queue for The Snow White and Seven Dwarves ride just as it reopened after the daily thunderstorm. We were here about 5 years ago when they were building this, and it was covered in scaffold (I had a scaffold company - went to the wall).

5 years to build a ride that lasts about 2 minutes? Mind you it must have been hard work for the dwarves so fair play to Mr Disney for sticking to equal opportunities.

As we came out of the mine, I noticed that there were quite a few folks dressed as Disney Characters. Now as we're into the last few days of the holiday, I'm just about getting used to this being the craziest place on planet earth, but the crazy that I witnessed over the next few hours was on a whole new level.

Men dressed as Mary Poppins.

Old women dressed as Tinkerbell.

Whole families dressed up like The Incredibles.

Kids dressed as animals.

I think one old woman in a mobility scooter had come as Roz from Monsters Inc. but she might just have been ugly and wearing a purple jumper.

What fresh madness is this? I had to ask a Cast Member what was going on and apparently it was a weekly event, catchily called "Mickey's Not So Scary Halloween Night", which was in turn cleverly shortened to MNSSHN (!)

 What?? It's August man!! Halloween is in **2 months' time**!

It's 100 degrees, me feet are melting into Mr Disney's tarmac and we're celebrating a made-up festival that's not until the end of October?

This was a nine on the Grumpy Richter Scale

Halloween obviously has a different meaning in the Sates – over here in the UK, we see it as a quaint pagan ritual where dark arts and witchcraft are celebrated in a slightly ghoulish setting. In the US, Halloween is seen as a free pass for all manner of perverts to fulfil their latent desires and fantasies, where men can dress as cartoon kids or women, hiding behind the excuse that they're doing it to get free candy or scare the fuck out of you.

And in any case, I just don't get Halloween. It really is **the** most stupid American thing, isn't it?

A bit like Proms, which seem to have totally taken over school life. The last year at Teenage Daughter's school was "all about the proms, dad". Teenage Daughter had to have "practice make up and hair", "real make up and hair", a £1000 dress and a ride in a Lamborghini! WTF! They're only kids!

When I left school in Dudley, you had your hair set on fire and had it put out by being pushed in the canal.

And that was the teachers.

Oh but of course, nothing screams Halloween more than a grown man wearing a home-made Buzz Lightyear outfit where he's coloured in a balaclava and made wings from an old cardboard box.

We carried on around Fantasyland with the goblins, elves, witches, princesses and blokes in drag - a bit like being in Wetherspoons in West Bromwich.

The highlight of the evening for me was when a rather bouncy lady dressed as Pocahontas decided to breast feed her newborn baby in the queue for the Winnie The Pooh ride. Nothing in my life has prepared me for the sight of a middle-aged woman dressed as a Red Indian squaw, flopping out a milky knocker on a kids fairground ride.

That image will never leave me. I can't unsee that.

We decided enough was enough and headed out through Moan Street USA. We'd seen enough crazy and it wasn't anything to do with the fact that Mr Disney wanted to charge me an extra $85.00 each to stay in a park I've already paid to get in. Honest. Not at all.

As we left I spotted that Mr Disney had set up extra security screening and there was a special section where all the men dressed as that little boy from Up had to hand in their dignity.

So back to Mr Disney's Convalescent Home For The Financially Crippled via The Marketplace Shop just in time to see my order for Mickey and Minnie's Stomach Stapling Kit had arrived.

Fell asleep dreaming of Mary Poppins. Which was nice.

Grumpy over and out

■■

Day 14 – Moving day

- ➢ Steps today - 6323
- ➢ Calories today - 6323
- ➢ Money spent today - 6323
- ➢ Number of times teenagers have moaned to me about writing these blogs - 27 today alone

The kids don't think these blogs are remotely funny or interesting (they think I'm turning into Alan Partridge just because I keep checking the likes on Facebook - "look love, Linda from Watford thinks I'm funny") and for once they're having a go at me for being on my phone. The irony! So I'm currently writing this with my head under the quilt.... ssshh don't tell them.

So, dear friends, this was Disney check out day for Grumpy but fear not as the madness continues for a few more days yet. Today, we would need to eat 16 meals (not joking) to complete the full set of Mr Disney's Dingo Dollar Dining Plan. I think it would be only fair if Mr Disney gave something back to everyone who completes the set, like a diabetes test.

We've got a bit irrational in the last few days, panic buying presents for ungrateful toddlers and getting those inspiring "quote a day" books to remind us of when we smiled once on holiday. And at the total opposite end of the scale, after spending enough money to start up a small business we've been rationing a £1.00 Home Bargains toothpaste between 4 of us for five days.

This is the day we all dread - packing for home. This is the day when us Grumpies criticise Holiday Mums for:

1. Bringing too many clothes ("how many pairs of shoes do you need?")
2. Buying too many gifts ("who's that for now?")

And in turn Holiday Mums criticise Grumpy Dads for not buying a good enough case from TK Maxx ("it was only £19.99 love. I know it's no good NOW..... please don't hit me).

At one point our bedroom looked like an emergency relief centre, with piles of clothes, carrier bags and kids toys everywhere. I half expected Sir Bob of Geldof to pop in and start filming a donation advert.

I wouldn't mind but I've worn the same 2 t shirts all holiday.

And women's toiletries! I've never seen so much chop slop, lotions, potions, pickles and sauces in my life. We've got more creams than Ben and Jerry's dairy.

This is also about the point in time when you start to regret buying that item of clothing you thought would be "lovely in Florida" but has still got the tag on. In my case, it's the white linen trousers and panama hat from Marks and Spencers. It'll look great in Dudley High Street.

In true family holiday fashion, Wifey and Grumpy bickered and rowed as the tension and clothes pile rises, while teenagers did really useful things to help. Such as completing an online driving theory test (Teenage

Daughter doffs cap) and watching more Alan Partridge videos (Teenage Son salutes cheekily).

To compound the chaos, there's frequent shouts of "Mum, where's me pants?", "Who's got the sun tan cream" and "Ooh Dad, Debbie from Guildford thinks you're hilarious. Ah-haa!".

All this unfolded as Teenage Son swaggered round in just his boxer shorts on his I-phone, stepping into the bathroom to do the longest and loudest piddle you have ever heard. It went on for ages and sounded like a fire hose bouncing off a shipping container. I think the entire landing must have heard as there was a spontaneous round of applause when he finished.

As the room slowly emptied into our luggage, including all the towels and Mr Disney's soap, there was a knock on the door and it was the maid. Perfect timing as we were struggling to zip the cases shut and she was a big girl. She spread-eagled herself on the first one and with the second she ended up joining the family in forming the kind of human pyramid that the Cirque de Soleil would be proud of.

One last check around the room to make sure there's no toiletries or peanut butter left and I headed off to get the hire car for our little rumble through Miami and a chance to listen to more country and western music.

I'd ordered the car through Dollar, and was mildly disappointed when I wasn't served by David van Day and the other girl. I used to have hair like that but mine was more Deirdre Barlow than New Romantic, and trust me that's not a good look in Dudley.

After seemingly signing my life away on multiple insurance forms, the friendly Dollar guy bought my car round to the front of the lot.

Oh my god.

I ordered a jeep, and ended up with a monster truck.

I think its called a Chevy Frankenstein and it is so big it comes with 26 air bags, 9 seats and it's own postcode. It's huuuuge. It's the only car NASA can see from space. If cars are meant to represent masculinity, well today my friends I'm Ron Jeremy.

I could have made my money back over the weekend by hiring it back out for funerals for big-boned people, or if anyone needed some Shetland Ponies shifting around.

When the fam got in it, the teenagers were fighting over which ROW they wanted to sit in and Wifey had to get a fireman's lift to reach the passenger seat. Wifey's only little ("I'm not short, I'm fun sized") and when she eventually clambered in she looked like the Dennis Waterman character off Little Britain ("write da feem toon, sing da feem toon").

Mildly disappointed not to find a gun turret, we had one last free refill and left Mr Disney's Residential Home For The Morbidly Impoverished, headed for Disney Springs.

I floored it as we went through the gate as I'd just managed to snaffle my own body weight in Twinings Tea Bags - in yer face, Mr Disney.

So off to Disney Springs Shopping Centre for the last chance to buy tat (thank god). They should rename this place Mr Disney's Mangle, cos it's his last chance to wring you out before you go.

We had a carb filled lunch at a restaurant called "Earl Of Sandwich", which is like Subway on acid, and then after a hot two hours of aimless plodding, poured the last of my spending money, ISA, runaway fund and the kids inheritance into a shop called Mr Disney's Top Pocket.

With heavy heart and lightened wallet, I climbed back into my monster truck and steered the fam out into the real world for a few days.

Coming up...... Stay tuned for the final adventures of Grumpy in Miami.....

Grumpy out

■■

Day 15 (and a cheeky bit of 14) – Pretend Rockets at Cape Canaveral

- ➤ Calories consumed - 65432 (tried all 4 cheesecakes - see below)
- ➤ Miles - couple hundred
- ➤ Astronauts met - 0

Hope you're all well and had a nice day / evening depending on where you are.

Picking up where we all left off yesterday, after I'd been strip searched by Disney security at Mr Disney's Mangle to make sure I had no cash left, me and the fam jumped up into our Chevy Frankenstein and drove to a place called The Cheesecake Factory. We hadn't quite reached our combined calorie intake for the day so a trip to a factory that makes cheesecake should get us over the line and give us a head start for next week. Apparently, this place is quite famous so we "simply had to go...."

The meal was all going ok until we got to pudding and I asked Smiley Waitress if they did a cheesecake by Sara Lee. As it turns out, they don't. But if I give them nine of my own dollars, they will make me a Peanut Butter Cup Fudge Ripple one.

Nine dollars!

That's 3 x Sara Lee's! Or 4 if I get them from B & M.

We ordered 4 "just to try" and 30 minutes later waddled out feeling sick.

And on to Cocoa Beach for 2 nights in a fleapit hotel before we go to Cape Canaveral to gawp at rockets.

I confess – I missed not being in Disney that first morning. No free refills, no lovely smells from the lobby and none of the staff called me Princess. And no Mickey Waffles, so instead we had to make do with an I-Hop (which I always thought was a bus service). Luckily, I-Hop do stacks of pancakes for breakfast that you can cover in syrup that will only take you 3 days to digest, so in we tucked.

With belly's full of eggs, butter and flour, off we wobbled to see the rockets. Apparently, Cape Canaveral is where they did all the stuff about pretending to land on the moon.

Yeah, I know. If you believe it then that's ok. But explain this to me clever clogs - if they can send 4 blokes in a tin can to the moon and back, why can't Dudley Council send some blokes round to fix that big pothole outside my house?

I rest my case.

Anyway, despite the charade, NASA (National Anonymous Secretkeepers Association) have built a lovely park with nice cafes, play areas and gift shops. They've even built a huge pretend moon rocket and stored it in a hangar, so people can see what it would have looked like if they could ever be bothered to get round to doing it.

The "rocket" was very convincing. It even had customised exhausts like the ones I got fitted to my first Corsa. There are lots of things to look at and loads of people from all over the world. I left The Fam to pop to the loo, just as a load of Chinese tourists were talking pictures of a bin and numpties queued up to touch a piece of "moon rock".

All this technology and the hand dryers weren't working! Hardly inspires confidence, does it? Come on guys, it's not rocket science.

Apparently, one of the main driving forces behind NASA's quest to explore space is to search out life on other planets. I can't help but think they've missed a trick here. I reckon I could have saved these blokes a fortune. As long as they pay their own air fare, I'll gladly drive them round West Bromwich where they would find all sorts of alien life forms.

Easy peasy - just park up outside Greggs and watch as the monsters, mutants and freaks walk straight from the benefit and re-emerge energised with a pack of 3 doughnuts and a steak bake.

A nice lady, who must have been clever cos she was wearing a white coat, was answering questions from a gaggle of schoolkids about the moon. I shuffled in to the group and politely asked her if we could look round the studio where they filmed the landings, but she quickly closed up her science briefcase and walked off. See? They don't want to admit it.

After a few hours of this we headed back to Cocoa Beach for a look round Ron Johns surf shop. This is a world-famous surf shop which is open 24 hours. Who's going shopping for a surfboard at 4 am? I've met surfers and they look barely awake when they're awake. Mind you there are lots of speciality shops in the US so why not a shop for nocturnal and insomniac surfer dudes? Righteous.

The shop is enormous, and they have something for everything that you'll never need. It reminded me of a shop in Dudley called Allan's. Allan made a living from selling everything on planet earth before Mr E Bay made it trendy or before Mr Aldi invented the middle aisle.

Part for a 1938 tractor? Allan had it.

Missing spigot for a Zanussi dryer? Allan has a set of them.

Moon rock? Allan has them in kilo bags, freshly scraped off the drive of Dudley Town Hall.

Allan had a long counter and if you asked him for something he'd disappear below it and after much scuttling, pop up 20 yards away like a meerkat with a multi pack of Russian flash wipes and a soldering kit for a Ford Fiesta. Allan sold tat from all round the world - if he'd put his mind to it, I reckon he could have given Mr Disney a run for his money. I don't think Allan was any good at drawing though.

I was tempted to buy some Old Guys Rule merchandise as it seemed to have just the right vibe for a Grumpy and the t-shirts were available in XXL, but Wifey soon put me straight on not wasting any of her holiday money.

As I've said before, I don't understand women at all. Not at all. But I have to concede that you are all brilliantly gifted and know exactly how to treat us Numpty Grumpies.

For instance, we were in the Chevy Frankenstein today, just pulling up to pay for parking by the rockets when I asked Wifey:

"Have you got any money?"

"Yeah, but it's in your pocket"

Even Grumpy thought that was genius.

So our day ended in an empty Taco Bell (*shudders*) as that's all I can afford. Although I did manage to snaffle loads of hot sauce sachets to go with me peanut butter.

Off on a road trip to Miami tomorrow so until then..

Grumpy out

■■■

Day 16 – Miami Bound

- ➢ Calories - 0
- ➢ Money left - 0
- ➢ Miles - I would walk 500
- ➢ Facebook Likes from Day 15 - 440 plus (thanks Grumpy fans, you're all mad)

After we performed our morning act of arguing over the bathroom, who made the toilet smell and what to have for breakfast, we checked our plans for today. This is our last full day so we're cruising the Chevy Frankenstein down to South Beach before I climb on board the big BA bird home (oooh that sounds rude! Sorry).

Actually, there is a new Fam daily routine - teenage kids like to troll my previous day's blogs, pointing out spelling mistakes, historical inaccuracies, loudly criticise any mention of themselves and admiring comments from fans (now known as Grumpettes).

"Ooh mum, Agnes from Cleethorpes sent dad 3 kisses. She looks nice. Look out mum, she might be a better cook than you".

Off we went, and as we spiralled down from the top of the multi storey car park, I got Frankenstein to do that squealy tyre thing that they always did on Starsky and Hutch and it felt really cool. I half expected David Soul to land on his bum on the bonnet when we got out.

On the road, it was time to set the touchyscreen Sat Nav. Frankenstein's Sat Nav is as big as the TV in our bedroom with icons that I will never need nor understand. Now I have a problem with touchyscreens. I reckon that when you become a Grumpy, your fingertips grow some sort of anti-touchyscreen laminated coating. It's probably from the same gene strand that makes Grumpy's nostril hair grow 5 inches every day and makes flaky wax constantly ooze out of your eardrum.

I've been befuddled by almost every contraption and gadget that you can operate with a touchyscreen. From phones to tablets, microwave ovens to plane TV screens, I've made myself look a complete muppet with my stabby, double and treble tapping which often leads to the opening of several (wrong) pages with a satellite delay and the screen covered in Grumpy Middle-Aged Dad finger grease. This is then quickly followed by exasperated groans from teenage kids, and quite often incorrect Amazon purchases (anyone want a Chinese Garment Steamer?)

The **Stubby Stabby Finger Dad Swipe** can be added to the long and growing list of things that I do that cause total and utter embarrassment to my kids. This list includes chewing loudly, clicking my fingers when I dance, putting my thumbs up to show satisfaction and talking to their cool friends without permission.

And this was the case now with Frankenstein's sat nav. Every time I entered a place name there was a 3 second delay that my brain wouldn't compute, leading to multiple spelling mistakes and shouts from the kids "Dad-uh.... fuh God's sake". It didn't help that I've not bitten me fingernails all holiday (I've never been hungry enough) so tapping any touchyscreen has been like stabbing glass with a knitting needle. It's took me ages to rite tgese bligs.

So we're on our way, cruising down to South Beach admiring all the mahoosive houses on either side. You know it's a posh area where you can't spot any smelly people and you see the drive thru for Kentucky Fried Swan. These stacks must have cost a fortune and I couldn't help wondering which one I would have bought if I hadn't just donated my life savings, the house and the kids inheritance to Mr Disney.

Sufferin' succotash we were hungry so stopped for lunch at a beautiful beach restaurant halfway down the coast, where I totally embarrassed The Fam by telling Smiley Waitress we were on the Disney Plan and we still had 6 credits left.

While I'm here, what is it with tipping in Humerica? Us Brits don't get it, do we? It's not in our culture and we're so stuck up our own bums in fright we don't know what to do.

Do we tip? How much? What if it's no good?

But it's their wages love.

It's not my fault there's no minimum wage.

You haven't left enough, cheapskate / you've left too much. Who'd you think you are? Richard Branson?

Humerican waitresses are good but us Brits like our servers to be more useless so it's easier to complain under our breath and write something horrible on TripAdvisor when we get home. We're far comfier with the bumbling incompetent indifference of Mrs Overall than the boppy, smiley get-it-all-right-first-time sun tanned Brandy from Vero Beach with cool tattoos and a hair braid.

Who was gorgeous by the way, lads.

So, on we merrily bopped through Vero Beach, where as it happens Mr Disney has his own exclusive Beach Club - if I hadn't been driving so fast and missed the turn, I would have popped in for a free refill.

I loved Disney, but this little road trip is proper Humerica and it is totally bonkers. I'm completely fascinated by the radio DJ's, the bonkers local news, endless weather updates and them big billboard adverts screaming out at you on both sides of the road.

"Doggers!! Where we got the best foot longs in all a Brevard County!"

I don't think "doggers" has the same meaning in The Black Country. I know of a park where dogging with a foot long would get you on the front page of The Dudley Chronicle.

"Visit Ol' Bob's Boot Scootin' Bar fuh the best in Country music".

This is another excuse for a Black Country joke:

Jack comes out of the Dudley country and western bar, clothes ripped to shreds, blood everywhere and covered in scratches.

'Arry says - "Bloimey mate , wor 'appened to yow?"

Jack - "the music's grayte aer kid, but I ay doin that lion dancing agen"

And country and western music.... there is nothing better for a Grumpy than miserable lyrics set to a jaunty upbeat tune with a fast picky banjo. I've decided to re-invent myself as a Black Country and Western singer (see what I did there?) when I get back home.

I'm going to update and re-release "Momma get the hammer (there's a fly on papa's head)" in a Black Country style.

Look out for "Mutha, get the omma, there's a wasp on the old man's yed" in all good record shops. And some bad ones.

On we boot scooted down to South Beach, singing along to country classics like " How Can I Miss You If You Won't Go Away?" and " You're The Reason Our Baby's So Ugly".

Yeehaaw!!!!

We reached our mega posh hotel on South Beach beachfront about 6 o clock, just in time for happy hour when I can buy a gin and tonic with an umbrella in it for only $25.00

The hotels ok but there's not many opportunities to increase my peanut butter rations. There's a different dynamic here - more organic, vegan friendly, dolphin hugging aloe vera juice than dandelion and burdock refills if you get my drift.

Finished the day drinking tequila sunrises as my eyelids sundowned, followed by organic burps and weird dreams about Mrs Overall.

Night night y'all

Grumpy out

■■■

Day 17 – South Beach

> ➤ Hangover - yes
> ➤ Paracetamols - lots
> ➤ Regrets about drinking tequila - hell yes
> ➤ Two thumbs "This Guy" jokes that annoy teenage kids - 25

I think me and Wifey overdid the tequila sunrises so apologies if this blog makes more sense than usual.

South Beach Miami is one hell of a place. If Disney is God's playground and Disco Cove his fish pond, then South Beach is where he hangs out with his mates at the weekend and gets wasted. We got here yesterday evening in time to see some people going out to party and others coming back from the beach, basically wearing the same clothes (or not, as the case may be. One girl wore such short shorts that as she walked it looked like her bum was eating them).

Here's another thing that us Grumpies don't get - valet parking. When the Chevy Frankenstein ground to a slow but majestic halt outside the hotel yesterday, I'd driven over 200 miles for around 4 hours, with the last hour through Downtown Miami like a scene straight out of Grand Theft Auto. But hey, for a bargain $45.00 per night, Ricardo can drive it a further 20 feet into the shade and put my handbrake on for me.

Wifey really liked Ricardo.

Grumpy paid the $45.00.

As the sun rose over the Atlantic sea heralding the start of our last day in Humerica, it bought with it the dawning realisation that in a matter of hours we'll be back home.

This made me very sad.

Instead of me and Wifey holding hands and loffin all the time, we'll be arguing about having the heating on, which colour bin it is and why I deleted 20 hours of Alan Titchmarsh programmes off the Sky planner even though we only had 2% left (is it me or is that bloke on every night? He's almost on as much as that ** shudders ** Claire Balding. I don't know why but she really scares me. If anyone reading this knows her, please don't tell her I said that).

I'll be back to the day job spending most of my time dazed and confused in Dudley. This time wearing my white linen trousers and panama hat but still with the customary Greggs sausage roll pastry round me stubble and three days nostril hair growth.

There won't be any thrilling rides to go on, no mahoosive meals and no heart-warming, tear jerking Pixar shows to watch. Instead it'll be back to tootling round garden centres looking at expensive Christmas decorations. Or even worse, following Wifey around "Vintage and Collectible" shops.

We do this a lot.

She ferrets round looking for an undiscovered gem, whilst I slowly pace around too frightened to break anything. I have no idea why, but every bloke I've ever seen in these places looks like me – an air of meek, cautious disinterest with the occasional "Oooh, that's nice love…." when your missus holds up an old farmer's welly that's been converted into a plant pot.

I imagine it's a bit like when Prince Charles is doing a walkabout on a hot Commonwealth island with natives dressed in chamois leather loin cloths.

I don't know how the owners of these shops get away with it, selling used toilet bowls as ironic sinks, antique Lionel Richie LP's and freaky looking stuffed animals who look like they croaked it just before they were hit by a car.

Who's got two thumbs and has mounted deer hooves as coat hooks? This guy.

And no more nicking condiments. Not because I can't but because I reckon I'm already over my luggage allowance and I'm dreading the thought of my case bursting open in customs and a gallon of peanut butter being smeared over my underpants. Well that's what I'm going to say it is.

I think my peanut butter scam has rubbed off on Teenage Daughter she went to the gym this morning and came out with 4 opples in her gym bag (apples to you poor non Black Country folk). I couldn't have been prouder. I reckon this holiday has turned me in to some sort of Black Country Fagin.

We couldn't hang around as we were heading to the airport, so we had a Smiley Waitress lunch by the pool (I ordered the crocodile sandwich and told her to make it snappy) and jumped up into Frankenstein for a last chance to listen to some country and western.

However, Ricardo must have retuned the radio in the 30 seconds he was in it as Barry Manilow was on the radio this time. I love Barry Manilow - me and Bazza have shared many a long car journey together. I've got my mum and dad to thank for liking Manilow. While all the other mods and skinheads in 1980's Dudley were in to The Jam and The Clash, I was having my hair permed, wearing tinted glasses and going to Barry Manilow concerts wearing a satin jacket.

I hope Claire Balding didn't read that bit or she might come round and duff me up.

Driving Frankenstein back to his multi storey rental home was quite sad. We had great fun together since being hooked up at Mr Disney's Granny Flats For The Financially Insane. I'll miss the smooth ride and superb visibility while Wifey will miss being transported around in a big leather armchair, diva pointing and pontificating as Humerica passes by her window. And being able to look down into other cars and stare at young bloke's legs.

We handed Frankie's keys to a young guy who told us we were heading out at the right time as Hurricane Irma might hit Miami by the end of the week.

That bought back some terrible memories of The Dudley Tornado from a few years ago.

Honest, there was one.

A tornado ripped through Dudley, whipping up the rubbish in the streets, tearing down smoking shelters and wiping out whole allotments. By the time it had finished, it had caused over fifty grands worth of improvements.

Tough times... schools closed, bingo halls cancelled the afternoon matinees and corner shops were boarded up. Total chaos. Some residents simply didn't know where their next scratch card was coming from.

By the time we'd emptied Frankie, we couldn't fit all the extra stuff in our cases - ironically it was Mr Disney's free refill mugs we were trying to fill up the cases with, so I suppose he had the last laugh.

So, we re-enacted that family scene that plays out at every airport check in, you know the one where you're still packing while simultaneously shuffling your case along the dirty floor, so you don't lose your place in the queue?

All four Hadleys assumed the position and offered our prayers to Samsonite, The God of Packing by kneeling over a case each, frantically re-sorting knickers, bras, souvenir mugs and peanut butter and repeating the mantra:

"doh show 'em me pants,
doh show 'em me pants,
doh show 'em me pants...".

We were all checked in and through security in no time, which left plenty of time to find the bar. As you know, dear reader, I'm not a big fan of flying so I need to consume my own body weight in vodka before I can get on board. An exaggeration, of course - it's become something of a mission of mine over the years to find the right balance between being happydopey where I'm everyone's friend and a total swivel eyed looney. I have been so scared of flying for so long that I honestly don't know what I'd do if I got on a plane without a vodka.

Last Black Country joke cos I'm boarding soon and in 10 minutes I'll be too pie-eyed to write anything.

Remember – breathe deep and channel your inner Noddy.

Noddy Holder walks in to a menswear shop:

Noddy: "Owroight bab. I'm gerrin Slade back tugetha. I need flares, platform shews, frilly sherts an top hats"

Bab: "Kipper tie, Noddy?"

Noddy: "Ar, milk an 2 sugars"

Oh, boarding now….

I'm ready to jump on the big BA bird (I know it's childish but I do like that joke, sorry. Us Grumpy's still snigger like kids when we hear "fanny pack") and to spend the next 9 hours breathing in other people's farts whilst trying to watch a film on the back of a postage stamp with me knees up by me ears.

Grumpy over and out

PS - please don't anyone tell Claire Balding I'm coming home.

■■■■■■■■■■■■■■■■■■■■■■■■■■■■■■■■■■■■■■■

Back Home - part 1 of 3

- ➢ Sleeps in own bed - 1
- ➢ Jet lag unexpected power sleeps - 4
- ➢ Number of times I've looked at the Disney App - 53

The flight home was fine, thanks for asking.....

Well fine if you're one of those thin bendy people able to contort your body into a shape that would allow you to slip effortlessly around a U bend. What dickwad tests these seats for comfort? I reckon those boffins from Boeing get little skinny kids as seat testers.

Or maybe that spindly little Gillian Mckeith has a pat time job sliding her little weak body in and out of test chairs. I don't like her.... you should always be suspicious of a woman who looks like a pickled scrotum who obsesses over poking your poo with a lollipop stick. By the way, you never see her and E.T. in the same room do you?

And what's the obsession with "extra leg room" on planes?

Why not extra "arse room" for people like me with a girthy bum?

What if you have a big body but only little legs?

How would Humpty Dumpty get on?

Through the door like everyone else......

(I'm boycotting emojis but if I was using them there would be a yellow smiley face right here ☞)

I also think you should have a button on your seat that makes the cockspangle in front shoot forwards. It should be at <u>exactly</u> the same speed that cockspangle shot himself backwards into my personal space without warning, causing me to colour in between the lines and knocking me gin and tonic over.

(Since I got back, I've designed and applied for a patent for the "Michael Hadley Aircraft Seat Cockspangle Button". It's in its early design stages at the moment as I'm trying to reuse a load of reclaimed Ford Cortina handbrake levers I've got lying around, but I'm hoping to meet with the eggheads from Boeing real soon. Keep ya posted....)

The "food" was served by a very handsome, dapper, polite young man. Don't you think the air crew guys always look like members of a boy band? Our guy today looked like that minor celebrity Ryland - beautiful white teeth, crisp tailored uniform and perfect facial hair that's been cut using a protractor and a surveyor's laser for 100% definition.

Ryland positively glided through the cabin with his size 28 waist (I save elastic bands that stretch further than that) with a twinkly smile and kind little comment for everyone. Mind you, it's a good job they banned smoking on planes cos he had so much hairspray, aftershave and fake tan if he were within 10 feet of a naked flame he would go up like a Christmas brandy pudding.

We arrived back in Heathrow to what Grumpy calls Grandad weather - cold, grey and miserable with the occasional unexpected little sprinkle. We collected the car and set off in the drizzle, bound for the M40 and the reality that this was the very last leg of the journey.

As we reached The Black Country we switched the radio to Noddy Holder FM to catch up with local news.

Wolverhampton has been twinned with the French town of Strasbourg, while Dudley has entered a suicide pact with Kabul.

For the third year running, Wombourne has won "Best Kept Village" while Bilston retained the title "Best Town in a Rear View Mirror "

Dudley Council has been rocked by a sex scandal after an official was arrested in Boots trying to buy viagra. He got caught out when the shop assistant asked:

"Am yo impotent?"

To which he replied

"Ar bab, oim the Mayor o Dudlaaay".

It was nice to be back home and rescue Molly the Cockapoo from her 2 week bumsniff ordeal round the old guy's house next door. As usual, Molly was fussed up by the fam whilst completely ignoring me... little bugger. I'm as popular with Molly as a fart in a jar of jam.

Wifey bought her a plastic, squeaky Mickey Waffle dog toy and it's just like the real thing - tough as a conker, completely indigestible and in a few days, will make a comeback in little yellow chunks in her poo. Now there's something for that Gillian Mckeith to poke a lolly stick at.

Within hours of our return, everything was back to Hadley normality and Disney seemed like a distant memory......

Both teenage kids turned back into their normal selves by managing to somehow <u>always</u> be standing in the way, usually with very little clothes on, filling the sink with dirty crocks instead of the filling the dishwasher which is literally UNDER THE SINK and getting frustrated when they don't get an answer as to where their clean clothes are within 3 seconds after shouting "Muuuum-uh" through four closed doors and a flight of stairs.

Wifey picked up where she left off before the holiday. Running around like a mad thing all day, burning herself out and eventually coming to rest in her usual position - hunched up with Molly the Cockapoo on the settee, furthering her career as a 10th Dan Candy Crusher whilst watching that cockwomble Alan Titchmarsh and his ugly mates dig up some old codgers garden.

As for me, I swiftly resumed my usual position in The Fam hierarchy. My natural place in the pecking order hovers somewhere between fresh bread and the lawn mower, depending on how long the grass is. I occasionally reach the giddy heights within the top three most important things in the household, usually as a result of being the only driver available or if Wifey has had a few too many the night before and needs a cup of tea and a bacon sandwich.

I also think my voice has gone again. It's really strange as I can still hear myself speak but everyone else doesn't seem to be able to hear me. It's the same as it was just before we left for Orlando - every time I say something no-one seems to take any notice.....

God, I miss Mr Disney

Sad Grumpy out

PS - That Claire Balding wasn't waiting on my drive so thanks for not telling her I'm back.

■ ■

Back Home - part 2 of 3

- ➤ Cups of Yorkshire Tea made - 8
- ➤ Central Heating level - up to 24 degrees
- ➤ Number of layers needed in bed - 2 + socks

It's difficult to stop thinking about my holiday with Mr Disney, even though we've been back for two days and we're still unpacking (where did all this stuff come from? I think we've accidentally picked up the luggage from a school trip)

I think the reality is I'm having trouble adjusting back into real life after spending 2 weeks at Mr Disney's Into The Light Residence For The Financially Demented. To be honest, not only is it difficult to adjust, it's difficult not to wish you were elsewhere (anywhere) when you live near West Bromwich.

I'm still dreaming of being in Orlando...... This isn't helped by being addicted to my phone, where I seem to spend an awfully long time reading fellow Grumpys' comments on Faircebuk (special Black Country edition, only available in Dudlaay).

It's not much fun when you're standing in a long queue at Greggs behind a young mum with an arse as wide as a car and kids competing in a screaming competition and you take a quick peek at your phone to see that Gary and Wendy just bagged a Fast Pass for Pandora.

I'm sure I'm not alone in this feeling – I reckon many other Grumpies have experienced the same come down after being bombarded with fun and happiness for two weeks, only to be bought back down to earth with a bump as soon as you get back home.

So, I've got an idea and as loyal followers of my blogs, I'm going to share this with you all.

I reckon Mr Disney should think about cashing in and creating "Disney Rehab" on all that spare land he's got knocking about once he's got rid of the alligators. He could invent totally new worlds more suited to broke, knackered guests like me, about to return home after 2 weeks eating, queuing, marching and spending.

I've given this some thought (there's not much else to do in Dudlaay) and I think I'm on to a winner here....... I know you're reading, Mr Disney so just drop me a friend request on Faircebuk if you want to meet to discuss it further and how you plan to pay me (don't accept Dingo Dining Dollars, sorry Walt)

So, here's my first draft plan for Disney Rehab:

Moan Street, USA - sponsored by Werther's Original

Gathering place for the GDAA (Grumpy Disney Addicts Anonymous). Hourly walk in self-help sessions, including special classes to complain about ungrateful kids, the price of a pint and how hot it is. Free refills of Sanatagen and Horlicks. Nightly candle parade featuring Disney characters such as Grumpy, Carl from Up and a special guest appearance by Yosemite Sam. (Cardigans and lap blankets supplied in bad weather)

****

Uncle Scrooges' Land Of Loan Sharks - sponsored by Wonga.

Multiple options for paying off your debt to Mr Disney, with expert advice on re-mortgaging the house, pawning the wife's jewellery and the best spots in Eastern Europe to sell your unwanted kidneys. Bonus attractions (seasonal) include classes on How To Benefit From Child Slavery and How To Compose Begging Letters.

****

Miss Piggy's Slimming World - sponsored by Weight Watchers.

Nutritional advice on how to cope with coming down to just 6000 calories a day, step by step eating plans for the re-introduction to real food like fruit and vegetables and salad preparation with the Swedish Chef. Urdeegurdee.

** Special bonus for 2017 - Dr Bunsen Honeydew's Gastric Band Clinic. Use your left over dining plan credits for a discount on Baloo's Stomach Stapling **

****

Mad Hatters World of Disney Addiction - sponsored by Methadone

Mr Disney's trained experts will guide you through detox treatments aimed at reducing your addiction to all things Disney. Patients will be limited to just 10 minutes per day of Frozen, and instead can choose from a range of Phil Mitchell documentaries or any show with Alan Titchmarsh (which is almost ALL of TV. Ever).

One to one counselling for Fast Pass Fever, helping GDAA patients cope with the failure to secure a family go at a convenient time on Flights Of Pandora.

** Limited Offer on Cruella Da Ville Sado Masochist Corrective Treatments. Buy a set of those sickly couples "Finish each other's..... Sandwiches" t shirts and get to burn them all. All of them. Please... Just burn them. All of them **

****

Thumper's World of Footcare - sponsored by Scholl

Footcare advice from Mr Disney's trained podiatrists to "Soothe and treat those achy feet". Special treatments available for fungal infections, corns and verruca's - blister popping a speciality. Come visit our interactive treatment rooms and see live demonstrations from Beaker on how to scrape off hard skin (goggles provided) and how we recycle the excess toenails into crispy onion salad topping.

****

Trust me on this.... I have a nose for a deal and I reckon I'm on to something here......

I'm going to keep developing this brainwave idea and if any of you Grumpy's want to join me and contribute ideas and, more importantly, hard cash, get in touch and together we'll pester Mr Disney for a high powered meeting in his big plastic castle.

If he's not bothered, we can always approach his nemesis, Mr Universal. I know he'll be up for a crazy idea - he's the guy still running the Extra Testicular ride 40 years after the film was released.

Looking forward to hearing from you Grumpies. I'm off now to design my park map....

Grumpy out

■■

Home - part 3 of 3. Grumpy's goodbye.........

- ➢ Number of times Alan Titchmarsh has been on my telly today – 6
- ➢ Takeaway meals since we got back - 4
- ➢ Footwear still on the landing:
  - Strappy sandals that all look the same to me - 8 pairs
  - Expensive teenage trainers - 6 pairs 1 odd one
  - Flip flops - 6 pairs

I swear it's like we took a millipede on holiday. Who needs all these shoes?

The fam pile them up at the top of the stairs like a big mantrap. I know they do it on purpose as I've seen the small print in my life insurance where there's special cover for being found dead at the foot of our stairs in the shape of the flag for the Isle of Man.

So, this is the end Grumpies. I can't keep blogging about Disney when I'm deep in deepest Black Country, so this is my last one.

Also, the kids lost all of the tiniest bit of interest that they had when they realised I wasn't going to be famous or make any money from it. They even got bored with calling me "Bloggit" and making suggestive remarks about Babs from Bristol sending me three kisses xxx. (Thanks Babs, see ya soon xxx)

And the only way I can persuade Wifey to read them is if I convince her that there's a secret, embedded code that unlocks a new level on Candy Crush or if I've added some pictures of Molly the Cockapoo.

For my last entry I thought I'd finish with a bang. I'll let you know a secret at the end of this chapter that will REALLY shock you.... but for now, here's what I've been doing to come down from 2 weeks at Mr Disney's "Staircase To Heaven Home For The Drastically Bereft".

I've been thinking about Mr Disney a lot in the last few days. He's a very clever man, and fair play to him and his team for doing so well.

But what's he got that I haven't?

Apart from a billion acres of prime real estate, centrally located in the sunshine state of the richest country in the world and a universal army of followers, there's not a lot between us really. And that got me thinking – why can't I do the same as Mr Disney? I can do exactly the same as him here in the Black Country, so I've been working on a secret plan to build Grumpy World.

More of that later.

In the meantime, I popped (or nipped, still don't know the difference between the two) to the world famous Merry Hill Shopping Centre, just on the outskirts of Dudlaaay, as I had to return my white linen trousers and Panama hat to Marks & Spencer before it was too late to get a full refund.

There's one of those big Disney shops at Merry Hill and I had a craving for a Mickey Waffle, so I thought I'd pop in to see if they had any spares or at least some cheeky Quick Snacks so I could use up the last of me Disney Dining Plan credits.

As it turns out, they don't sell Mickey Waffles, Quick Snacks and they can't even give me a free refill!

But what they have got is a big security guard from Smethwick called Darren who's very good at twisting your arm up your back, lifting you up off your feet and dropping you on the floor of the Merry Hill car park.

After a considerable length of time wiping off car park dust from my trousers and trying to get my elbow back into place, I headed into Marks & Spencers to get my full refund for the white linen trousers / panama hat stunning combination.

Is there anything worse than being patronised by a hipster?

The young guy handling my refund had his own look, even though he was only working behind the till at Marks's and almost certainly broke all the uniform rules. He had a trendy beard, multiple leather bracelets and a trendy pair of glasses that he probably didn't need. He looked the kind of guy that would drink ultra skinny lactose free lattes with his hipster mates, discussing vegan rights and praising Jeremy Corbyn.

He was a right tosser.

He squeezed out every drop of patronising joy as he handled my refund. Looking at me, looking down at the now pathetic looking white linen trousers, then looking back at me with a thinly disguised hipster smirk.

I felt bad enough, before he went on to say:

"Reason for the return? I'm guessing they didn't they fit, sir?"

It was as much as I could do not to jump over the counter and pull his head down by his little wispy hipster beard on to a chubby thrusting knee.

Instead, I giggled nervously and said, "Ha, yeah something like that, too much holiday indulgence…." whilst patting my belly and winking.

Tosser.

On the way home, I popped in to Dudlaay Council with my application to build Grumpy World on the vast wasteland right next to the town centre where Woolworths, C & A and Tandy used to be. I reckon the timing is perfect with the amount of people wanting to take their holidays in Disney, but not being able to afford the ridiculous cost due to the exchange rate and the fact they can't be arsed to travel. My plan is to bring some Disney / Grumpy magic by basically copying all of his ideas but in a Black Country style.

For those of you that know Dudlaay, we've already got a head start. For instance, we already have:

Our own castle (could be Magic Kingdum)
Our own zoo (easily as good as Animal Kingdum)
Our new modern bus terminal (mirror image of Epcot)
Our own Black Country FM (passable resemblance of Hollywood Studios. If you squint)

We also have a collection of fine restaurants and entertainment outlets to keep all the family happy - Mecca Bingo, Wetherspoons, Wimpey and a brand new Toby Carvery - as well as mega retail outlets like Poundland, B & M and a really big Lidl.

We've also got numerous funfairs that regularly tour the Black Country, which will be handy for extra summer labour and when we need all the new car parks tarmacking.

And if that wasn't enough, we have our own "Dudlaaay Oye" (Dudley Eye) where for just £10 a go you can sit inside a glass pod smelling of wee and kebabs and spin effortlessly above the famous tatty skyline of the Black Country's capital city. Get a scruffy pigeons' eye view of such delights as the abandoned gas works, the disused sewage farm and the derelict sanitorium.

At 10.37 am (Dudley time) all the folks on the scrounge would be able to Fast Pass the benefit queue so they've got more money and time to spend in Threshers. Although I am thinking of putting it back to 11.45 after the Jeremy Kyle show has finished. I've even thought about seeing if there's a way I can convert their probation tags into Magic Bands, so we can speed up the queueing process.

And if all that wasn't enough, once we've fished out the shopping trollies and old cars, we can use the local canal network as a lazy river. I've secured a deal with the local Kwik Fit for all the old inner tubes so there's almost zero cost involved there.

I addressed the application letter to Mr Mayor himself as he's a Mason and I know he's "well connected" to loads of local building firms. So, fingers crossed all you Orlando addicts will have no need for your Disney fix in a few years' time, and instead of jetting off to Florida at massive expense, you can get the replacement bus service from Birmingham New Street, right into the heart of Grumpy World, the Home of Black Country Magic.

Look forward to ~~fleecing~~ seeing you.

Now for the big reveal……..

The secret is I'm not <u>really</u> Grumpy at all.

I'm actually quite.....

Ermmmm….

How do I put it.....

Happy.

And I'll tell you why.

Orlando is amazing. And Disney World Florida is quite possibly one of the happiest places on earth.

Yes, it's expensive.

Yes, it's hot.

Yes, it can be stressful.

But it's also one of the most magical, enchanting places on Planet Earth. I dare you to name any other place where whole families can be bought together in an atmosphere of pure joy and love, where children can experience such delight and wonder, and where dreams really can come true.

Take a look at some of the thousands of online videos where kids are being told they are going to Disney for the first time, toddlers meeting Minnie Mouse or marriage proposals in front of the Magic Castle and see for yourself how Disney brings joy and happiness into the lives of millions of people each year.

Each park is full of happy kids, all having the time of their lives, surrounded by people that love them and care for them. Whole families spending time together, all feeling the same love for each other (just stop to think for one minute and consider how rare that is in the crazy, turbo speed life we all live).

Disney is an incredible organisation. It raises millions for charity, helps educate on global warming and is totally inclusive in its policy of recruitment. The incredible staff represent a total cross section of all of us. Partially able, young and old, folks from different ethnicities from all over the world are there to ensure that guests have a magical time and feel completely at home.

I moaned and complained a lot while I was there, but in truth I would go back in a heartbeat if it meant that I could spend just one more precious moment with The Fam.

And that makes me Happier than you can imagine.

Thanks for reading. It's been a blast. And in the words of Mickey Mouse himself....

That's all folks!

Afterword

Dear reader, thank you for coming on this journey with me. If you've read this far, right through to the end, I am truly grateful. This is the first book I've ever written, and it's been great fun from daft beginning to emotional end. If you are like me and have always had an ambition to write a book but didn't know where to start, DO IT! DO IT NOW!!If a chump like me can do it, then an even bigger chump like you can.

This book was cobbled together from the daily blogs in Orlando, and due to the reaction it received, took on a whole life of its own. As I came toward the end of the blogs and decided that I could somehow turn the mad rantings of a Grumpy Middle-Aged Dad turned into an actual book, I took inspiration from the many charities that do amazing work with Disney, and kids in general. In order to really give myself a kick up the arse and complete the job, I decided to self-publish and donate the proceeds to charity, which in turn will help unfortunate kids as they and their parents struggle through their own journey.

Through my own blog page, I asked for charity nominations and I was totally overwhelmed by the response. In all, more than 15 different charities were nominated and it really was a tough choice to make as every single one is a worthy cause. In the end, I've decided to go with two main charities as both fitted the bill - I wanted them to be UK children's charities, and have some connection to Disney or Orlando. Ideally they would be "less well known" charities that fight harder than others to raise awareness. I hope I've made two good choices....

Charity number one is **Follow Your Dreams** and was nominated by my new It's Orlando Time friend Zoe Hamonda. It's a UK charity based in South Wales that supports children with learning disabilities, some with life-limiting medical or severe developmental conditions. Follow Your Dreams inspire the ambitions of children and young people by delivering enjoyable methods of learning and play. They do incredible work and I would urge you to please go to Facebook and like and share their page.

Follow Your Dreams was a popular nomination and is a great cause. I came to this choice after speaking to Zoe, who helps out as a part time volunteer at the charity. During the course of writing the book, Zoe trained for and completed the Cardiff Half Marathon in aid of Follow Your Dreams, despite having **no marathon experience** AND recently **overcoming a mini stroke.** Superhuman or what? Zoe is exactly the reason why these charities survive – simply by blood, guts and determination and helped me make it easy to decide to choose Follow Your Dreams.

The Neuro Foundation is charity number two and this one is really close to all the followers of It's Orlando Time. There was a fabulous holiday blog completed by Joshua Draper, who's mum Emma took them all on holiday with little brothers Oliver and Daniel, and dad Michael.

With his mum's help, Joshua completed a daily blog of their family escapades in Orlando, and it was really well received by all on It's Orlando Time. Joshua's back story is that he suffers from Neurofibromatosis Type 1, which not only causes tumours to grow on nerve endings but leads to learning difficulties. Despite this incredibly tough start to his life, Joshua is a brave lad and managed to blog every day about his family's holiday in Orlando – if you haven't seen them I urge you to go on It's Orlando Time and search Emma Draper.

The Neuro Foundation is the authoritative voice of Neurofibromatosis in the UK. They achieve this by providing first class information, support and advice; facilitating and promoting innovative research, and being an advocate for those with Neurofibromatosis. They also raise much needed money to support on-going research in to the disease.

As I write this, I'm speaking to both charities about the best way this book can be turned in to cash for them – the fact that you are reading the book suggests that you are a generous person, and have already given some of your own money to them. For this, I thank you from the bottom of my heart and you will truly be blessed with good fortune throughout your life.

On the other hand, if this is a second hand or borrowed copy and you haven't donated, shame on you. Reader, you have a chance to rectify this quickly by sending some money to either charity.

If you don't, I'll send Acting Harry Potter round and put a *Sectumsempra* curse on you.

Printed by Amazon Italia Logistica S.r.l.
Torrazza Piemonte (TO), Italy

41341155R00096